Niagara Falls Ontario Book 1 in Colour Photos, Saving Our History One Photo at a Time

Photography
by Barbara Raué
©2018

Series Name: Cruising Ontario

Book 207: Niagara Falls Book 1

Cover photo: 5938 Corwin Avenue, Page 16

©All the photos in this book have been taken with my cameras. I own the rights to them.

Series Name: Cruising Ontario
Saving Our History One Photo at a Time
in colour photos

Books Available in Alphabetical Order:
Aberfoyle, Acton, Ajax, Alton, Amherstburg, Ancaster, Arthur, Auburn, Aylmer, Ayr, Beaver Valley, Belgrave, Belleville, Bloomingdale, Blyth, Brantford, Brockville, Burford, Burlington, Caledon, Caledonia, Cambridge, Carlow, Chatsworth, Clifford, Collingwood, Conestogo, Delhi, Dorchester to Aylmer, Drayton, Drumbo, Dundas, Dunlop, Eden Mills, Elmira, Elora, Erin, Essex, Fergus, Goderich, Grimsby, Guelph, Hagersville, Hamilton, Hanover, Harriston, Hespeler, Jarvis, Kingston, Kingsville, Kitchener, Lake Superior, Lincoln, Linwood, Listowel, London, Lucknow, Merrickville, Mono, Mount Forest, Mount Pleasant, Neustadt, New Hamburg, Newboro, Newport, Niagara-on-the-Lake, Oakville, Onondaga, Orangeville, Orillia, Oshawa, Owen Sound, Palmerston, Paris, Pelham, Perth, Peterborough, Petrolia, Pickering, Port Colborne, Port Elgin, Portland, Preston, Rockwood, Sarnia, Sault Ste. Marie, Seaforth, Sheffield, Shelburne, Simcoe, Smiths Falls, Smithville, Southampton, St. Catharines, St. George, St. Jacobs, St. Marys, St. Thomas, Stoney Creek, Stratford, Thamesford, Thunder Bay, Tillsonburg, Toronto, Waterdown, Waterford, Waterloo, Welland, Wellesley, West Flamborough, Westport, Whitby, Windsor, Wingham, Woodstock

Book 198: Chatsworth
Book 199: Wingham
Book 200: West Flamborough
Book 201-202: Whitby
Book 203: Ajax, Pickering

Table of Contents

Corwin Avenue	Page 5
Culp Street	Page 17
Main Street	Page 31
Ferry Street	Page 41
Sylvia Place	Page 44
Barker Street	Page 44
Summer Street	Page 51
Lundy's Lane	Page 52
Lowell Avenue	Page 61
Peer Street	Page 62
Fallsview Boulevard	Page 64
Robinson Street	Page 65

Niagara Falls Ontario is located along the Niagara Falls waterfalls and the Niagara Gorge on the western bank of the Niagara River, which flows from Lake Erie to Lake Ontario. The Niagara River flows over Niagara Falls at this location and creates a natural spectacle that attracts millions of tourists each year. Niagara Falls is about 130 kilometres (81 miles) by road from Toronto, which is across Lake Ontario to the north.

Louis Hennepin, a French priest and missionary, is believed to be the first European to visit the area in the 1670s. Increased settlement in this area took place during and after the American Revolutionary War, when the British Crown made land grants to Loyalists to help them resettle in Upper Canada and provide some compensation for their losses after the United States became independent. Loyalist Robert Land received 200 acres and was one of the first people of European descent to settle in the Niagara Region.

Tourism started in the early nineteenth century. The falls became known as a natural wonder, due in part to paintings by prominent American artists such as Albert Bierstadt. Niagara Falls is the self-proclaimed "honeymoon capital of the world."

With a plentiful and inexpensive source of hydroelectric power from the waterfalls, many electro-chemical and electro-metallurgical industries located there in the early to mid-20th century.

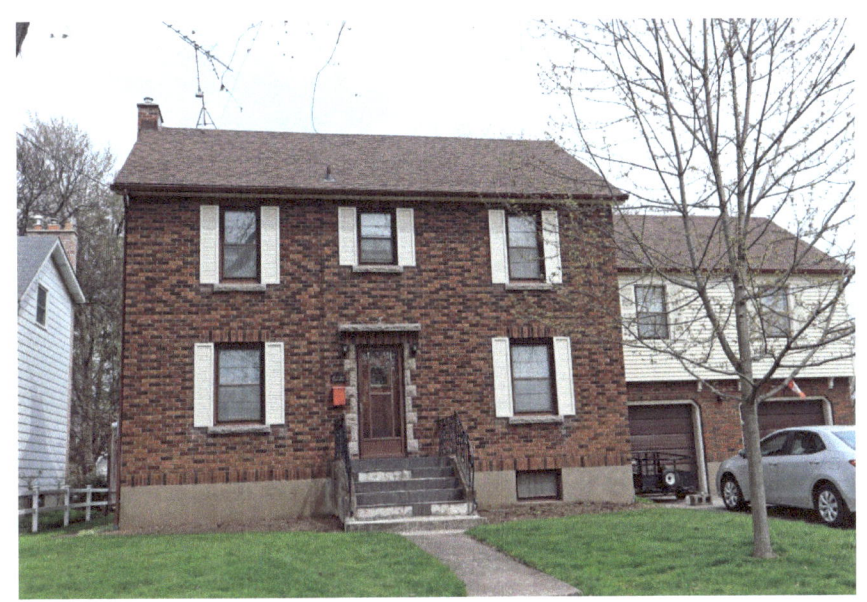

6220 Corwin Avenue

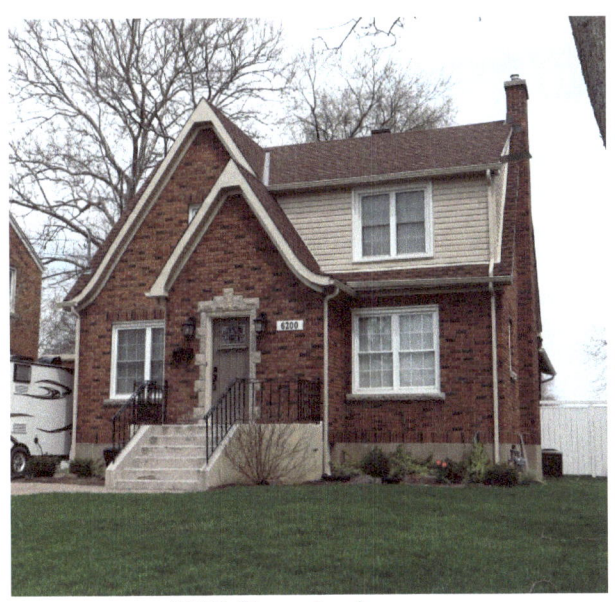

6200 Corwin Avenue

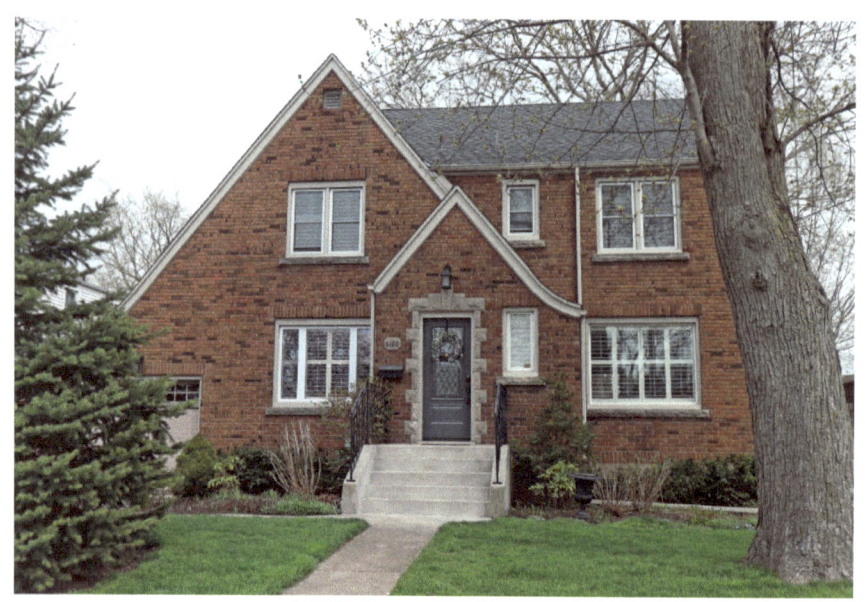

6180 Corwin Avenue

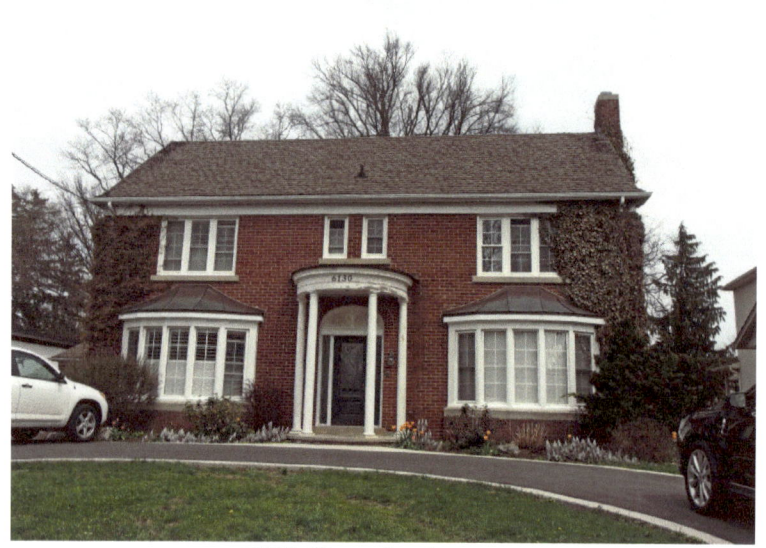

6130 Corwin Avenue

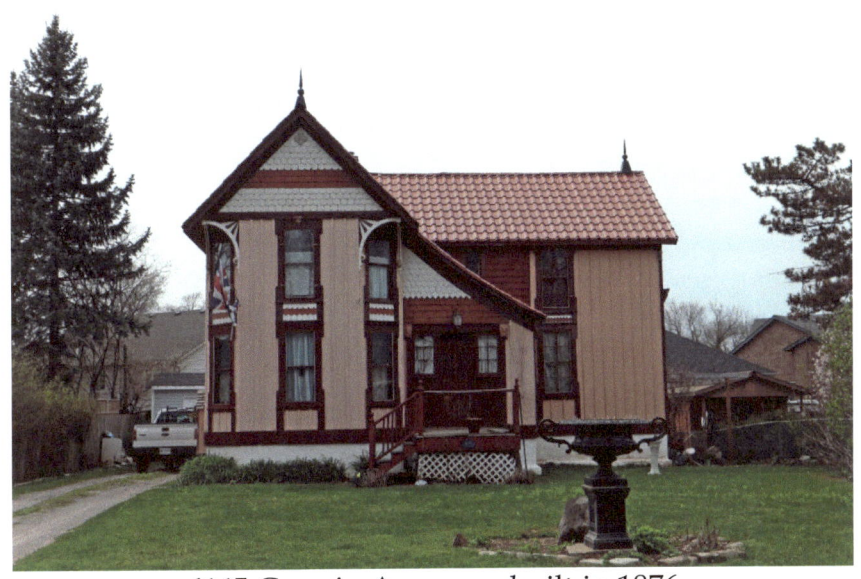

6145 Corwin Avenue – built in 1876

Egerton Ryerson Morden built and lived in this house. He operated a successful nursery on ten acres of land that surrounded his home. He specialized in small fruit plants and ornamental trees. The house is an example of board and batten in the Italianate and Stickley styles. It has an irregular "L" shaped plan with a one-story kitchen and bedroom addition to the rear. It has patterned wood shingles and ornamental roof brackets. The house was relocated from Dorchester Road to Corwin Avenue.

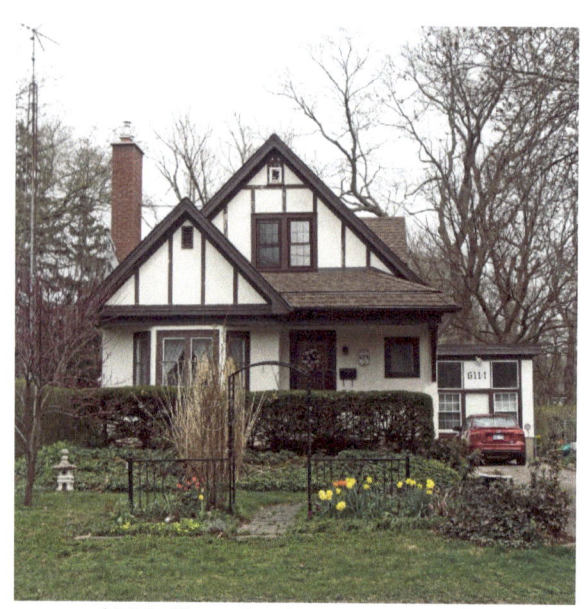

6114 Corwin Avenue - Tudor

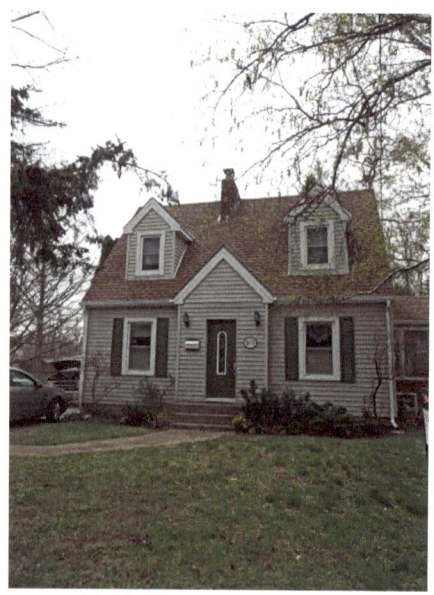

6113 Corwin Avenue

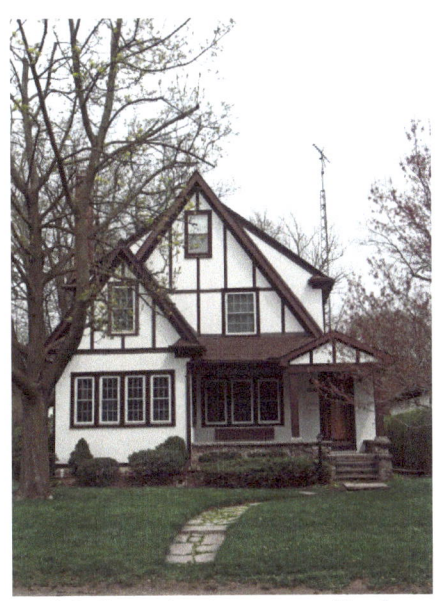

6106 Corwin Avenue - Tudor

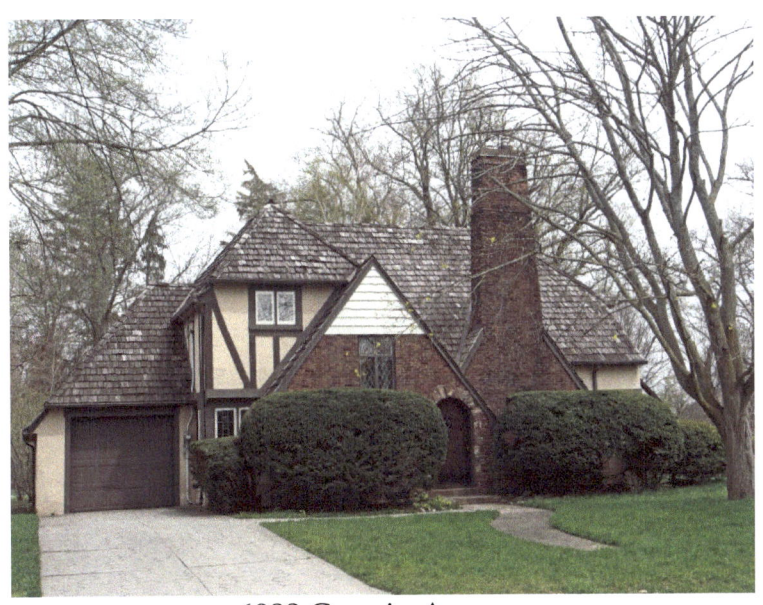

6088 Corwin Avenue

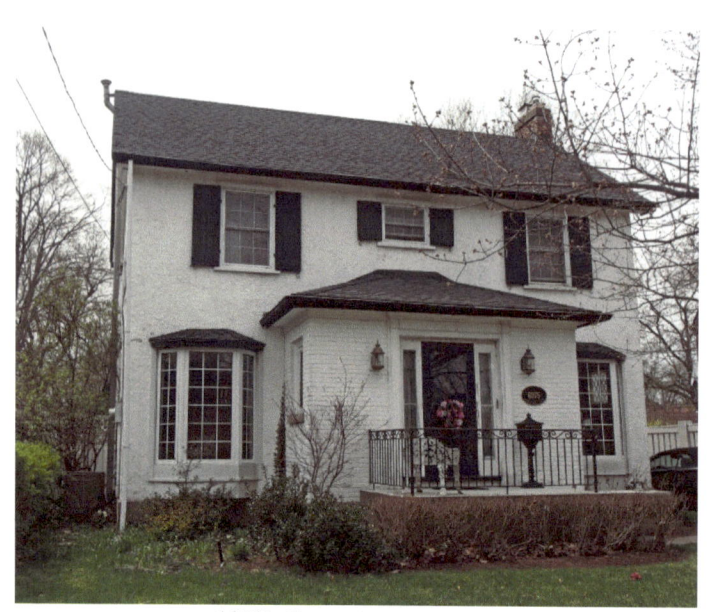

6075 Corwin Avenue

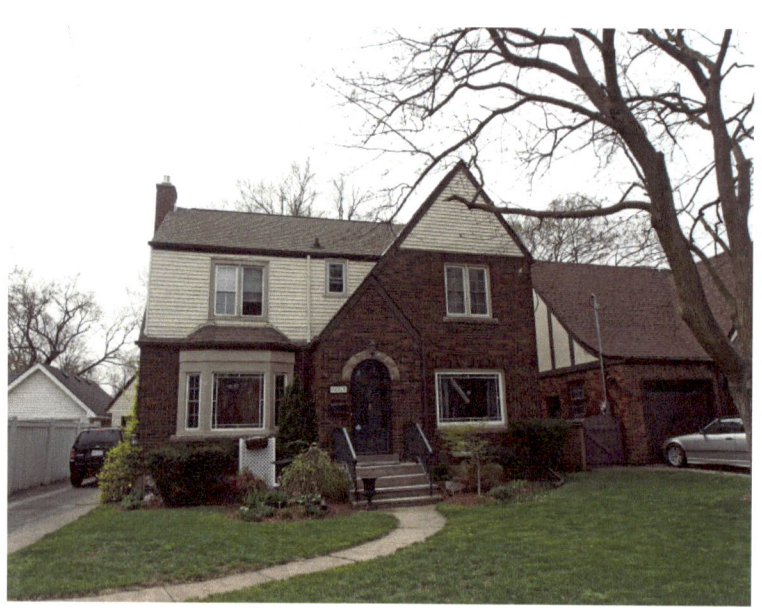

6063 Corwin Avenue

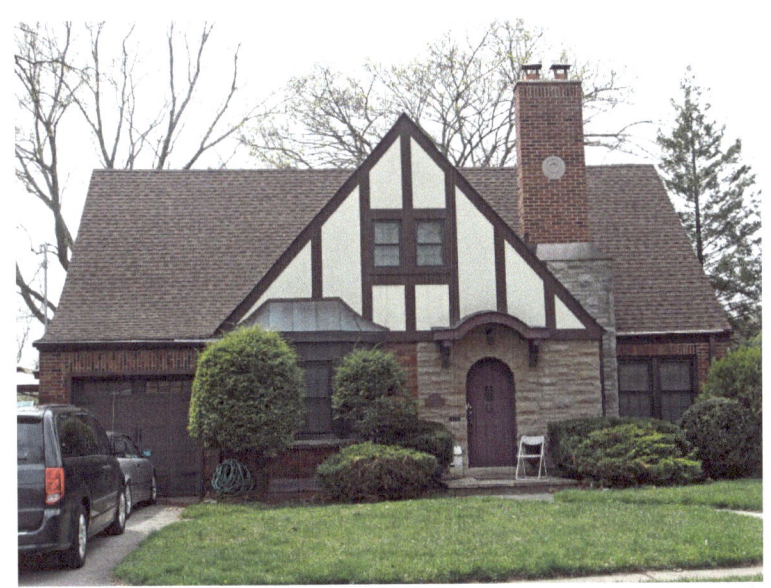

6055 Corwin Avenue Tudor

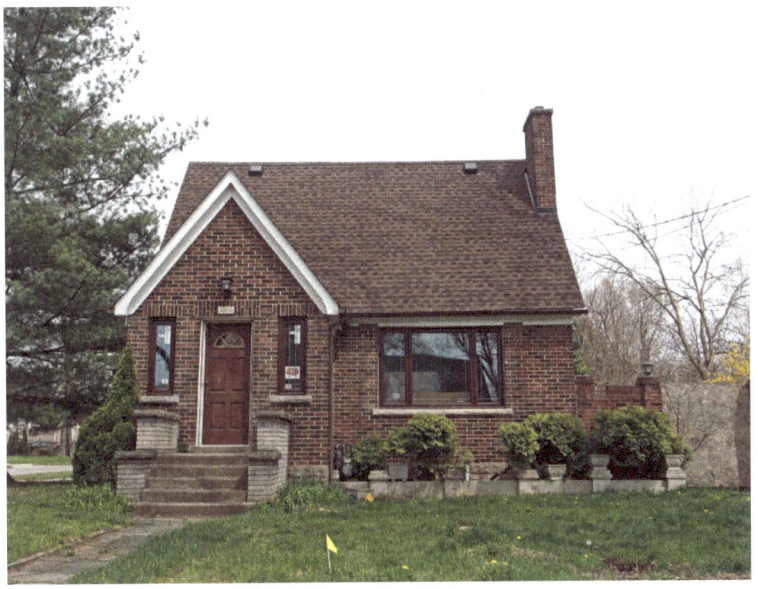

6054 Corwin Avenue

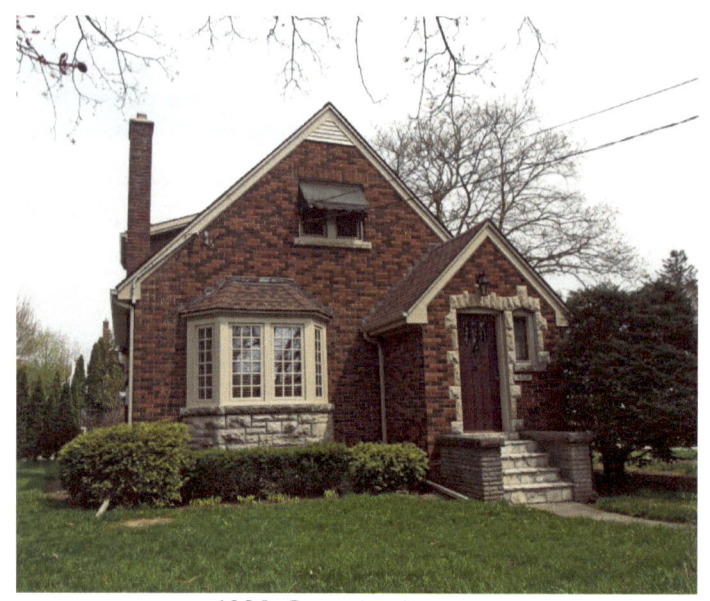
6028 Corwin Avenue

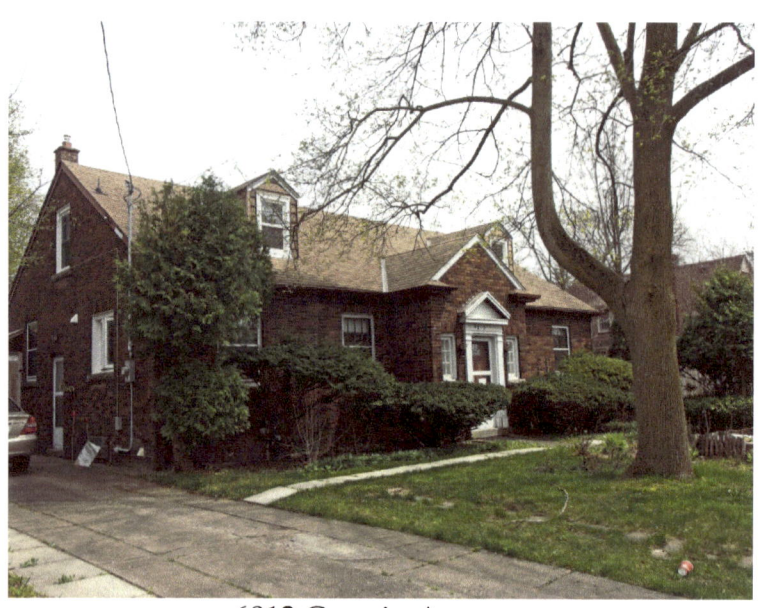
6012 Corwin Avenue

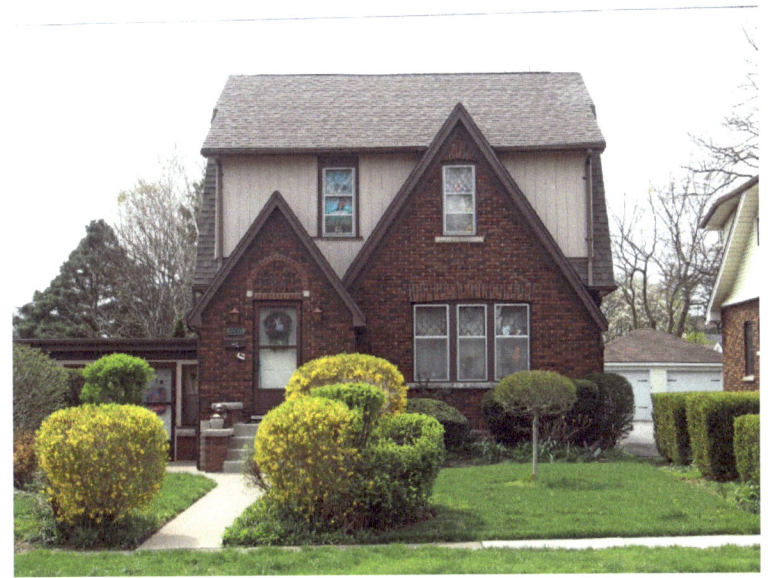

6005 Corwin Avenue - Vernacular

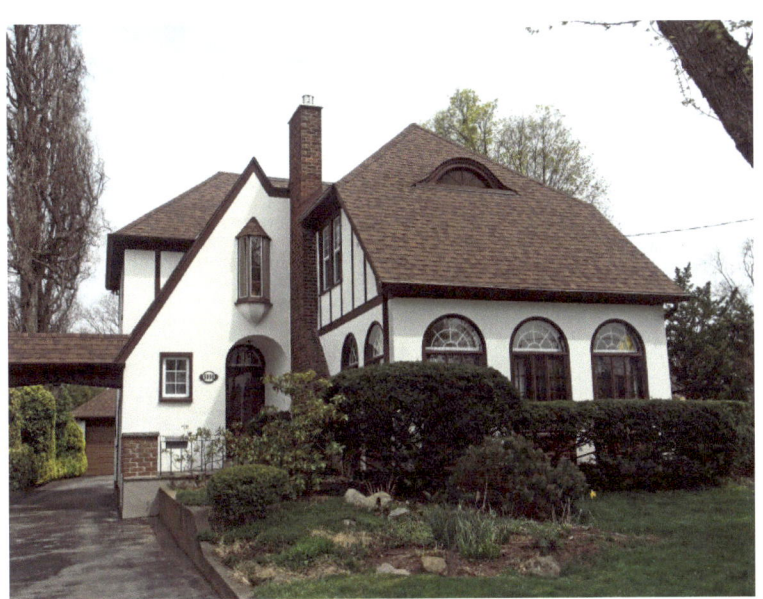

5998 Corwin Avenue

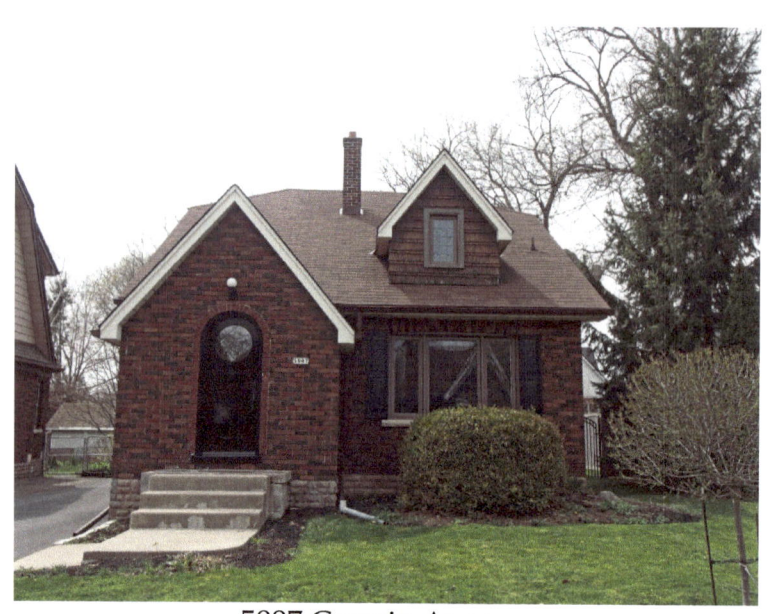

5997 Corwin Avenue

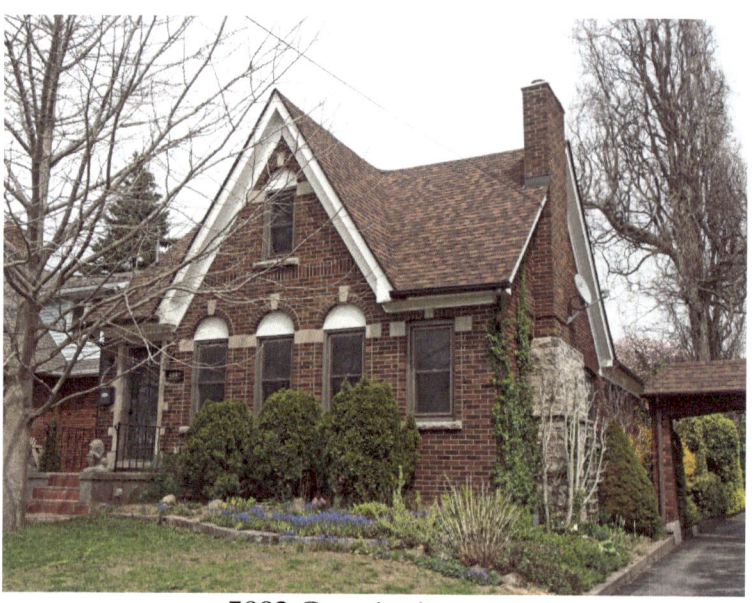

5992 Corwin Avenue

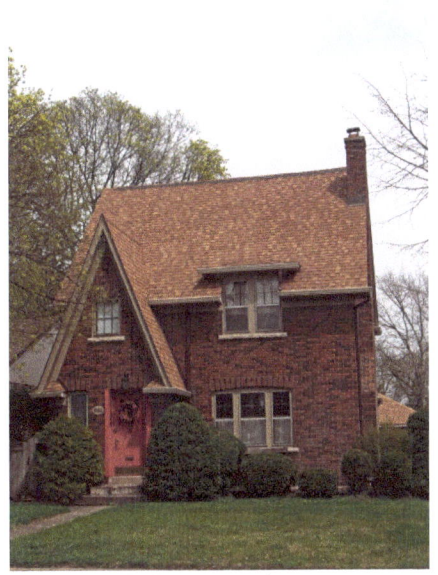

5962 Corwin Avenue

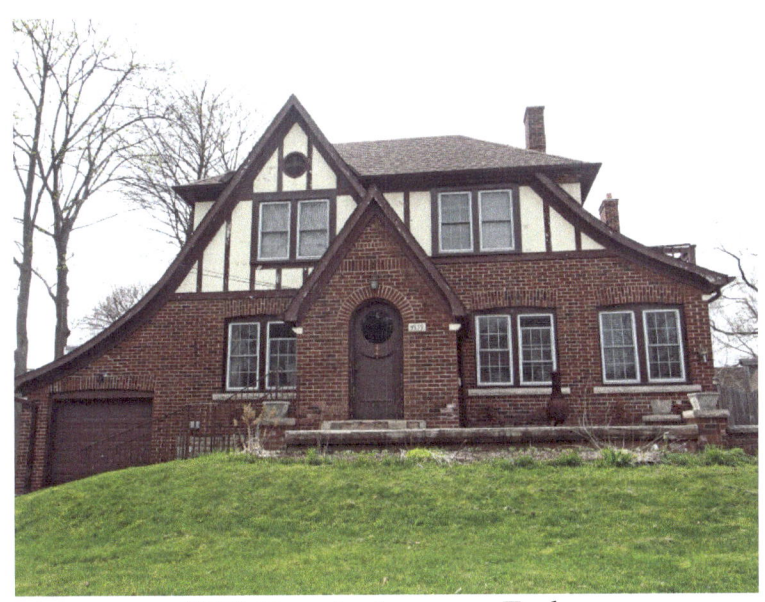

5959 Corwin Avenue - Tudor

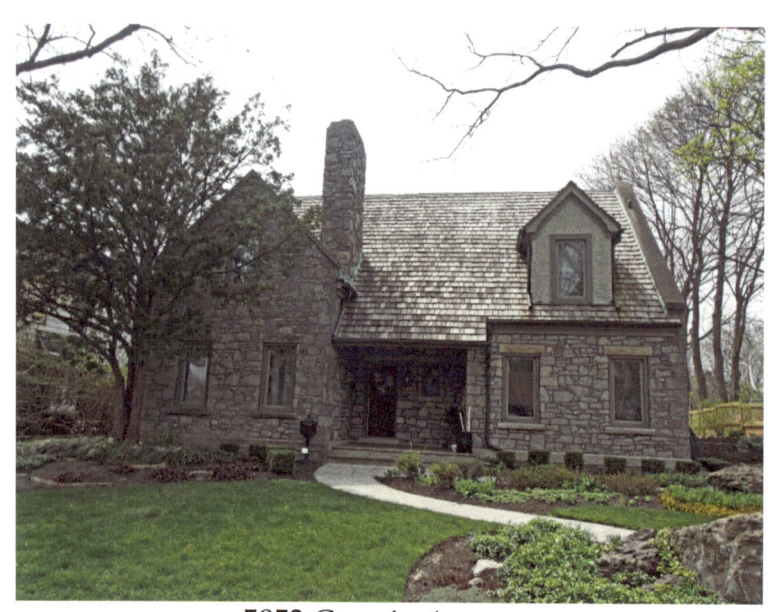

5953 Corwin Avenue

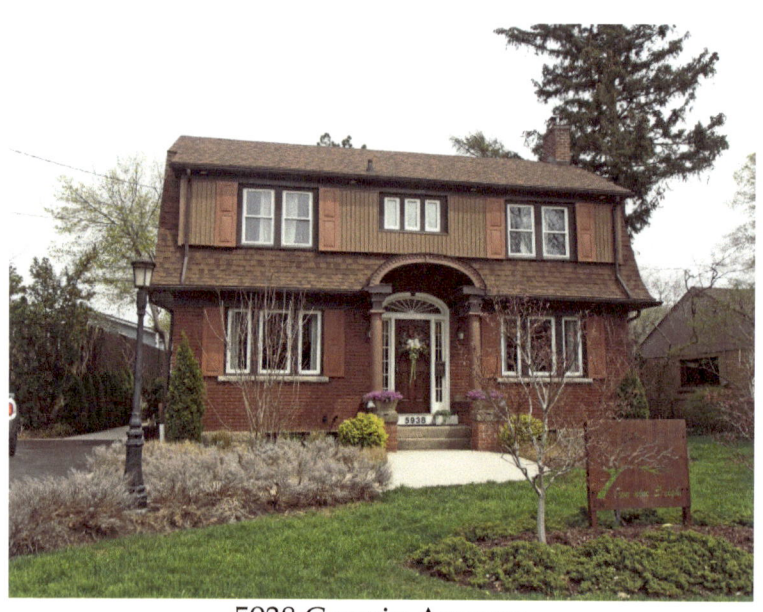

5938 Corwin Avenue

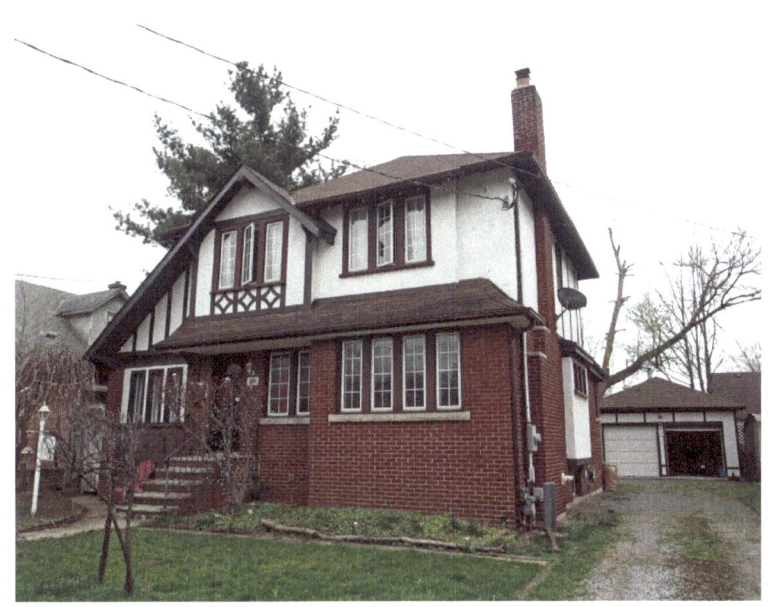

6184 Culp Street - Tudor

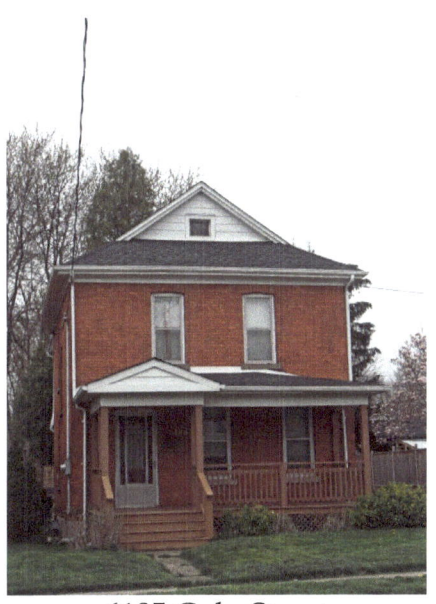

6185 Culp Street

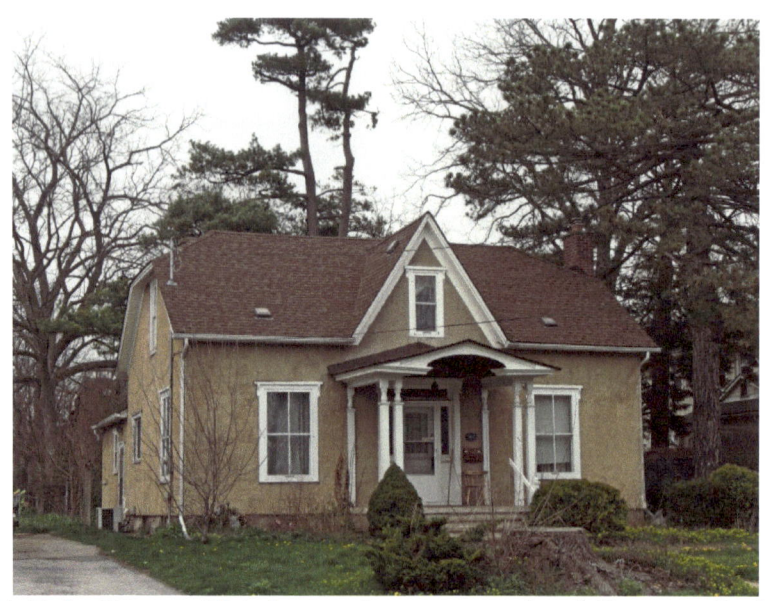

6151 Culp Street - This house is an example of Cottage Gothic and was built in 1855. It has a central peaked gothic gable and a jerkin head roof (a roof having a hipped end truncating a gable). The windows have simple wooden drip caps. The central door opening has a transom and sidelights.

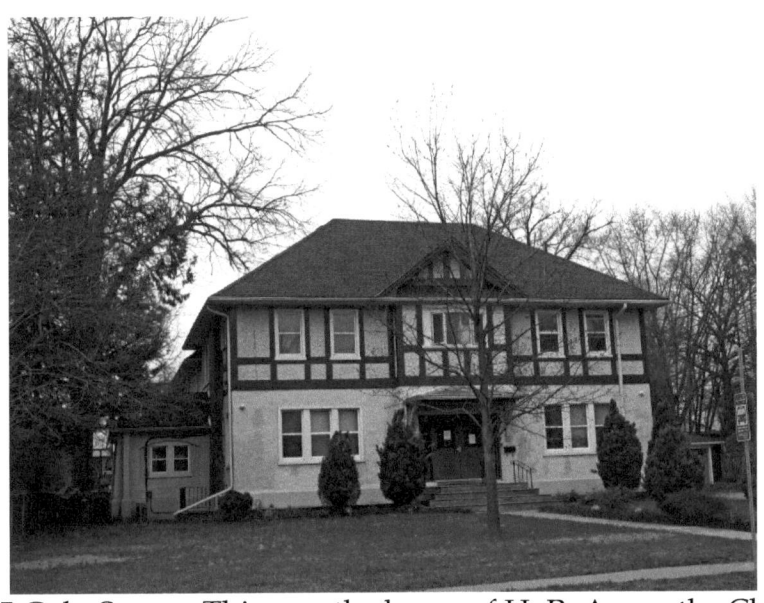

6135 Culp Street - This was the home of H. R. Acres, the Chief Hydraulic Engineer for the Sir Adam Beck Generating Station No. 1. The Tudor Revival style is shown with its exposed wood beams. The central bay projects forward and is surmounted by a central pediment in the roof. The front entrance is protected by a roof supported by brackets. The front entrance has a double door with sidelights.

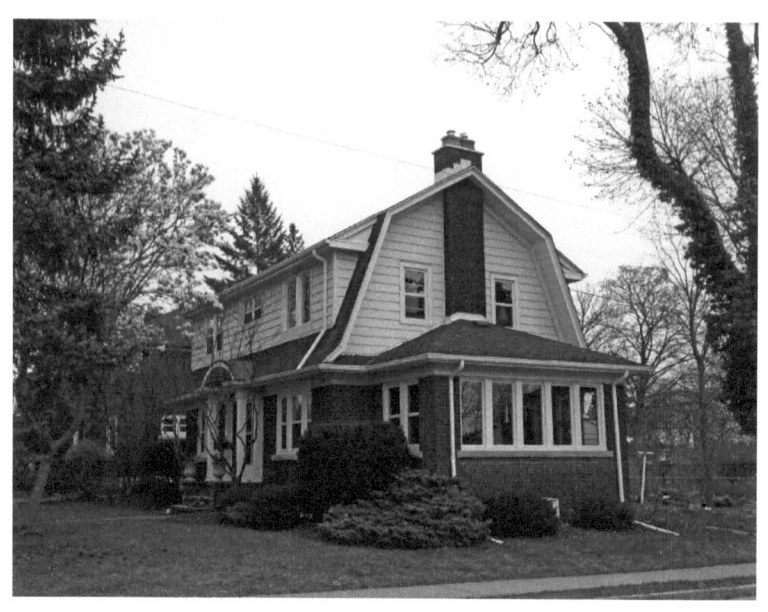

6140 Culp Street – Neo-Colonial – gambrel roof, shed dormer

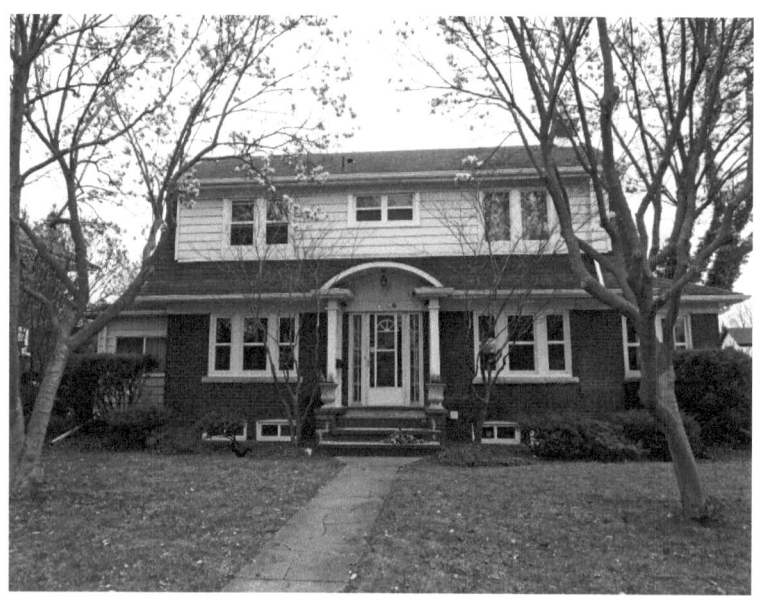

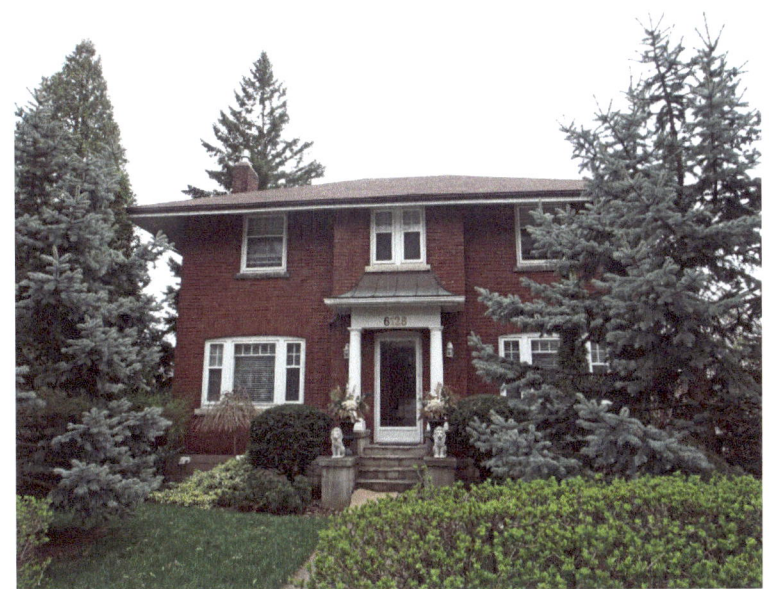

6128 Culp Street

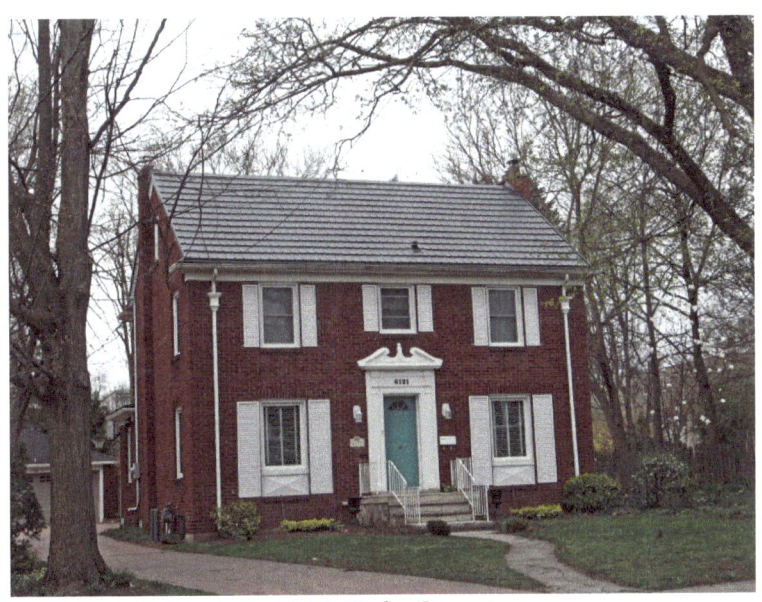

6121 Culp Street

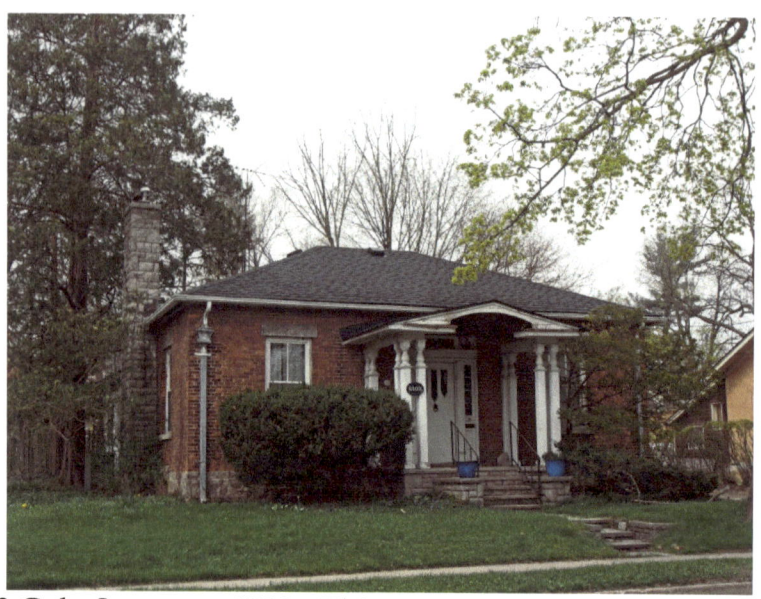

6103 Culp Street – c. 1798 - This was James Forsyth's second home in Drummondville. His first was located on the site of St. Mary's Ukrainian Church. Forsyth was one of the first ten families to settle in this area in 1783. For many years Isaac Culp owned the house and farmed the surrounding land. It is in the Regency Cottage style in a square plan with a low hip roof and symmetrical arrangement of openings across the front façade.

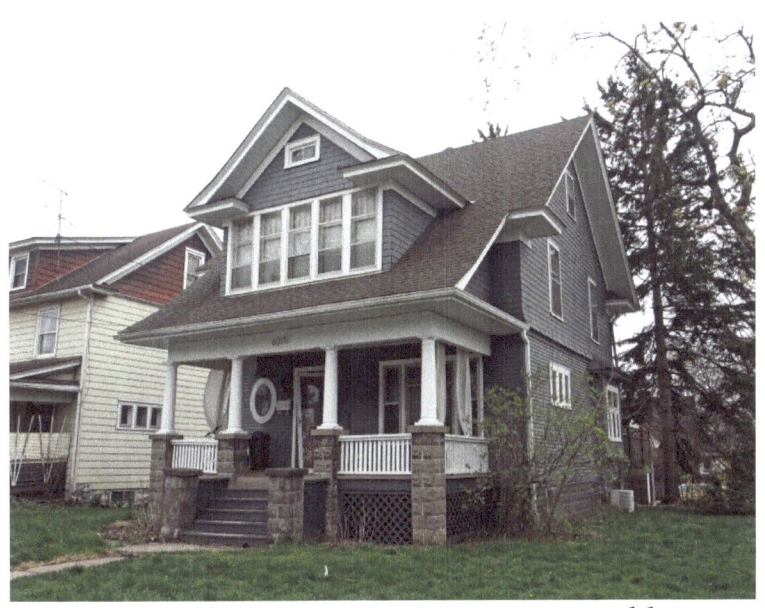

6078 Culp Street – cornice return on gable

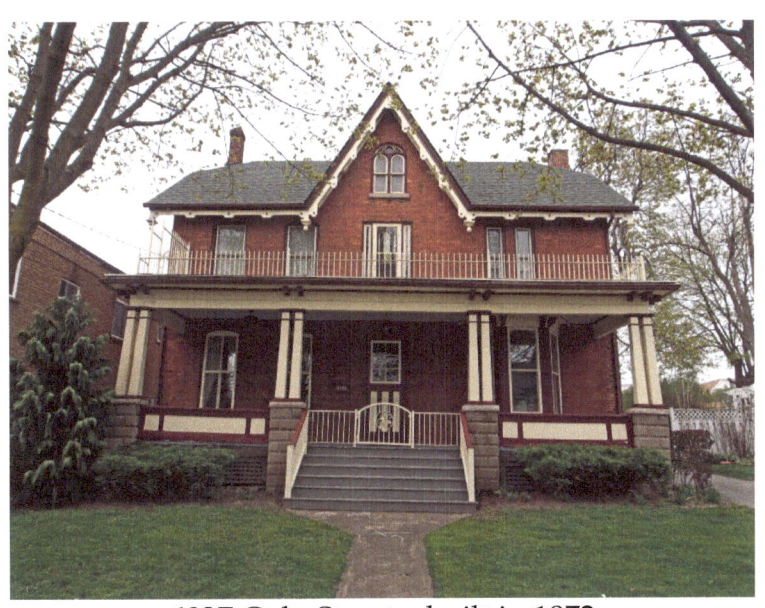

6037 Culp Street – built in 1872

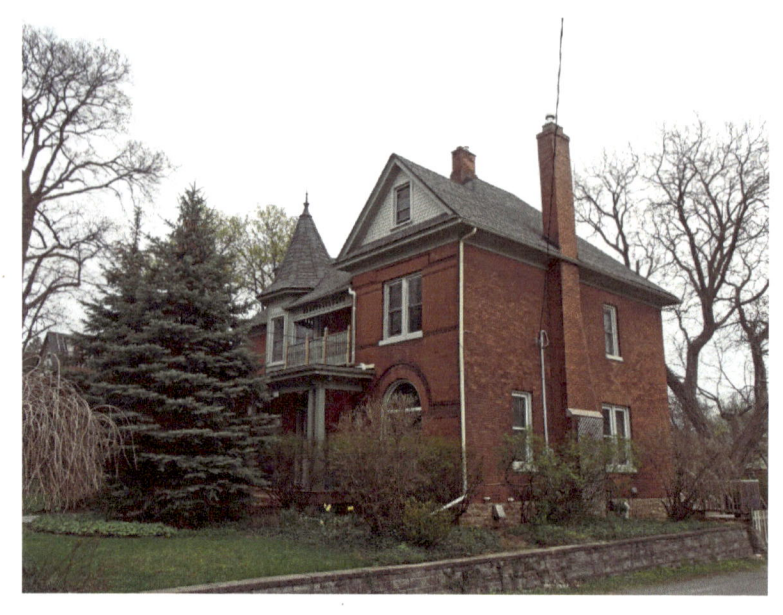

6028 Culp Street

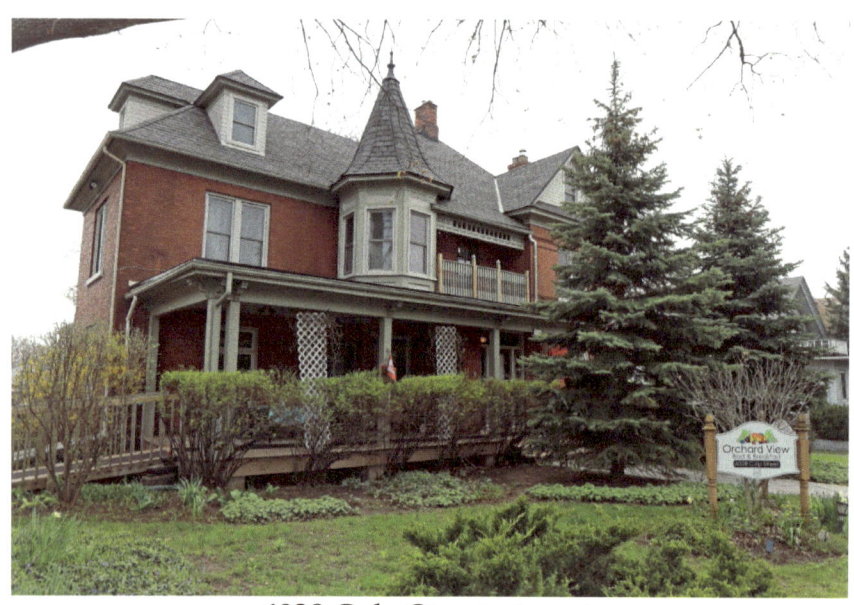

6028 Culp Street - turret

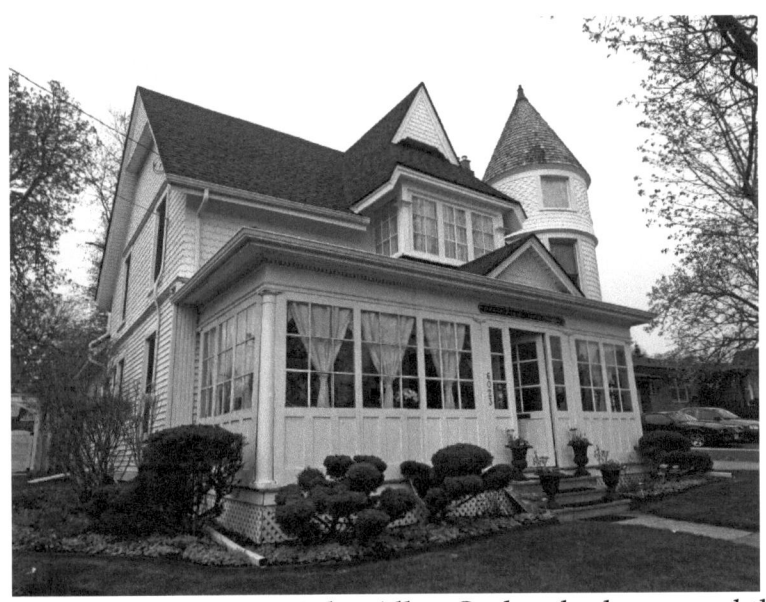

6023 Culp Street - John Allen Orchard who owned this house was a prominent member of the Drummondville and Stamford Communities. He came with his father from England in 1836. He purchased Lot 5 on Culp Street in 1856 and the house was built soon after. He served as Township Clerk and Clerk of the Division Court. His nephew Joseph Cadham lived there after his uncle's death in 1896. Joseph's daughter Margaret inherited the house and lived there the rest of her life.

This house has many features of the Queen Anne Revival style. The house has both decorative and wood shingle finish and clapboard siding. The tower and verandah were probably added later in the 1890s.

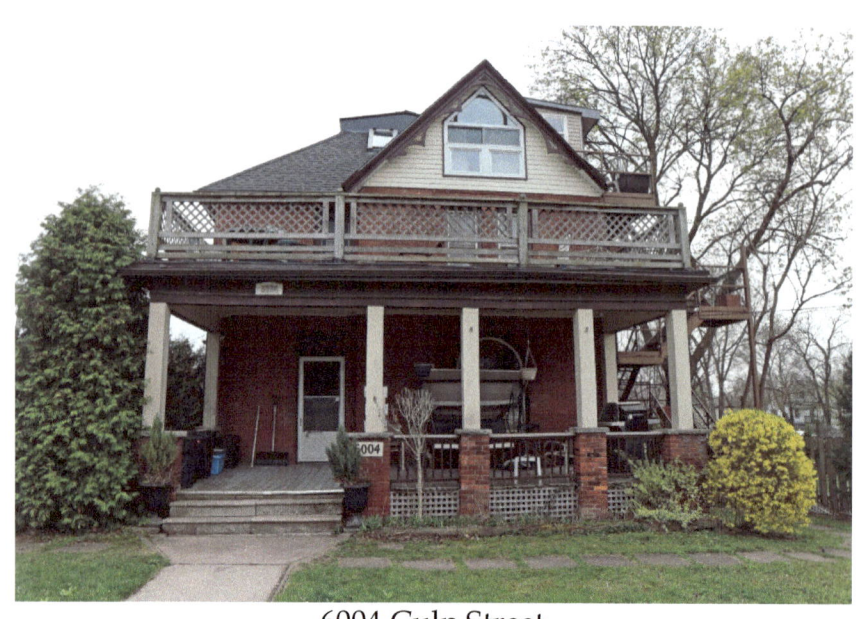

6004 Culp Street

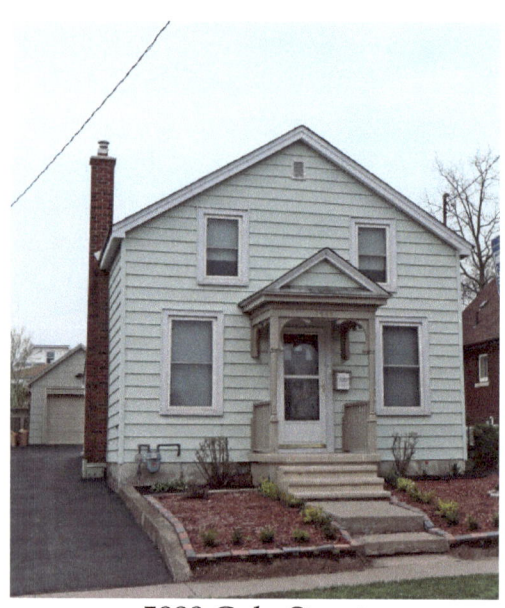

5999 Culp Street

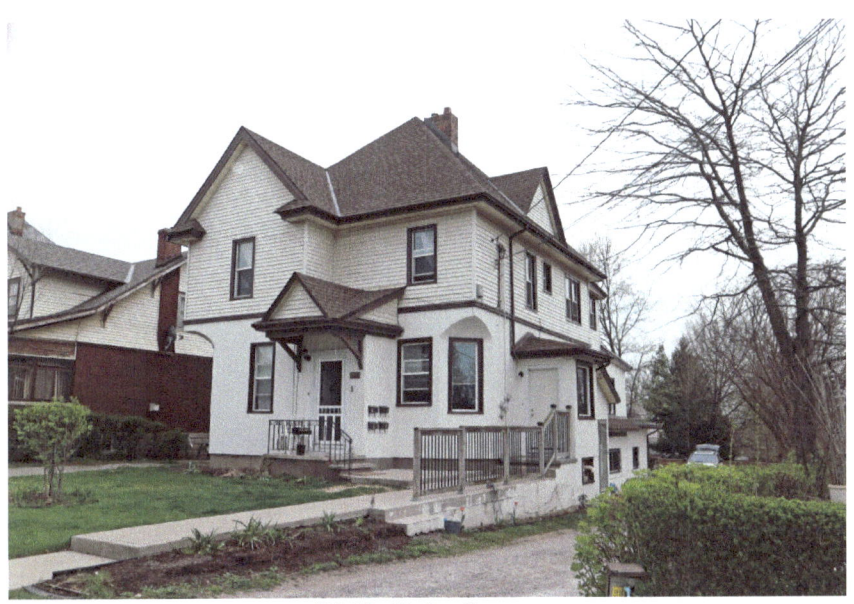

5962 Culp Street

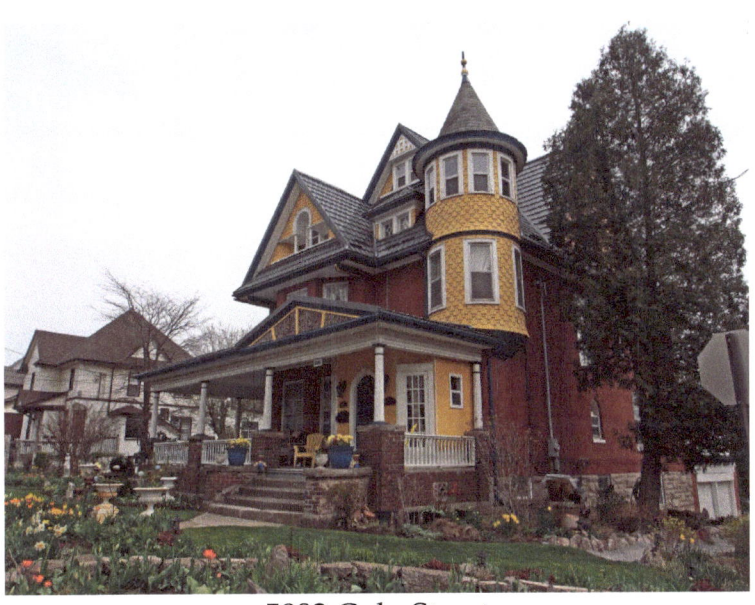

5982 Culp Street

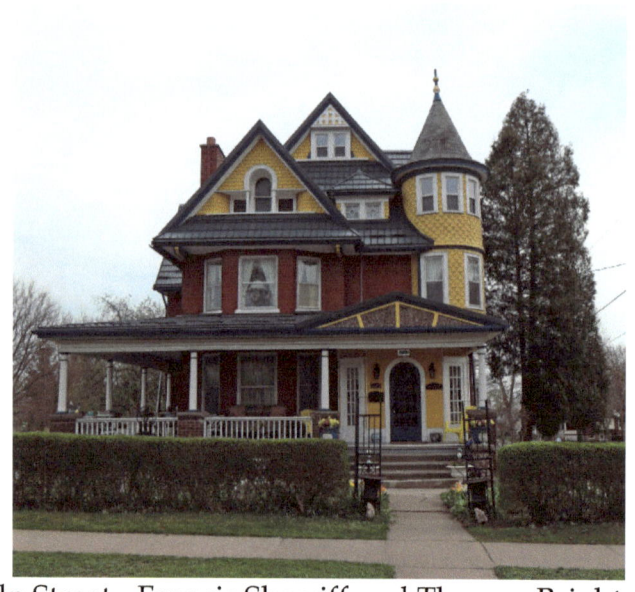

5982 Culp Street - Francis Sherriff and Thomas Bright started the *Niagara Falls Wine Company* (Brights Wines) in Toronto in 1874. They moved to Niagara Falls in 1890 to be closer to their major source of grapes. This house was built for Francis Sherriff in 1894 for a cost of $4000.00. It is in the Queen Anne Revival style with an asymmetrical form, deep porch, and an irregular roofline which includes gables, dormers and a turret. The house exterior is brick with decorative cedar shingles on the turret and in the gables. The three-part window in the front gable is an adaptation of the Palladian style; the central section has a round headed window. The large wraparound porch has Tuscan style columns that rest on a brick base topped with a square stone cap.

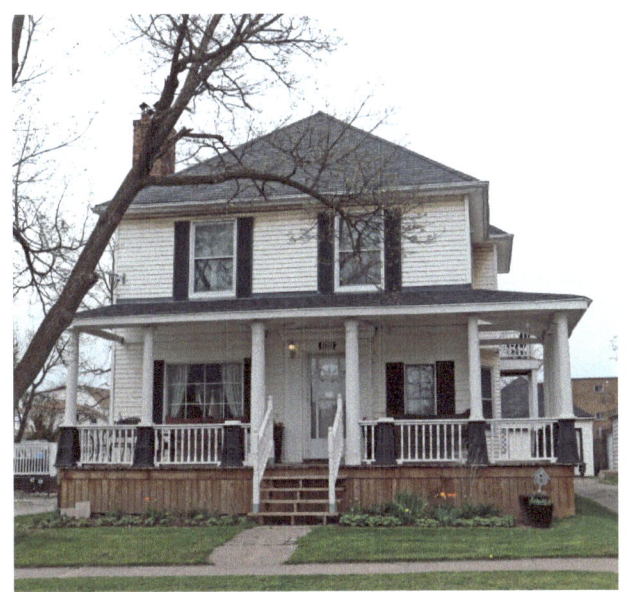

5969 Culp Street

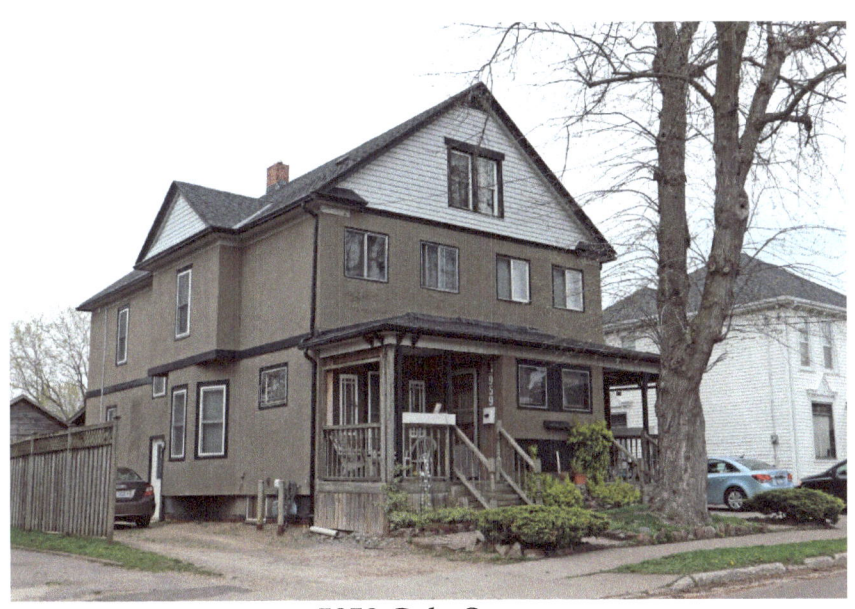

5959 Culp Street

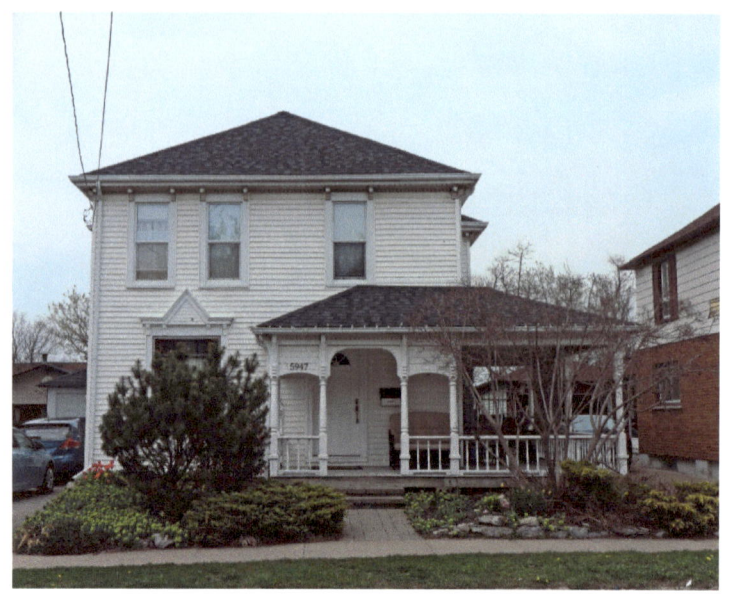
5947 Culp Street – hipped roof

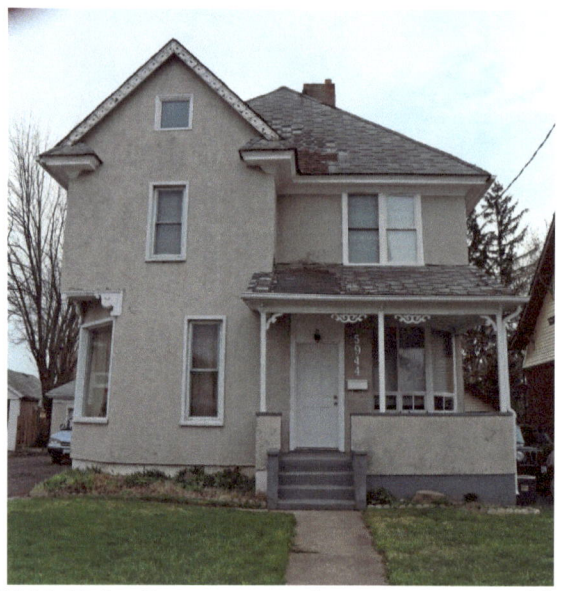
5944 Culp Street – cornice return on gable

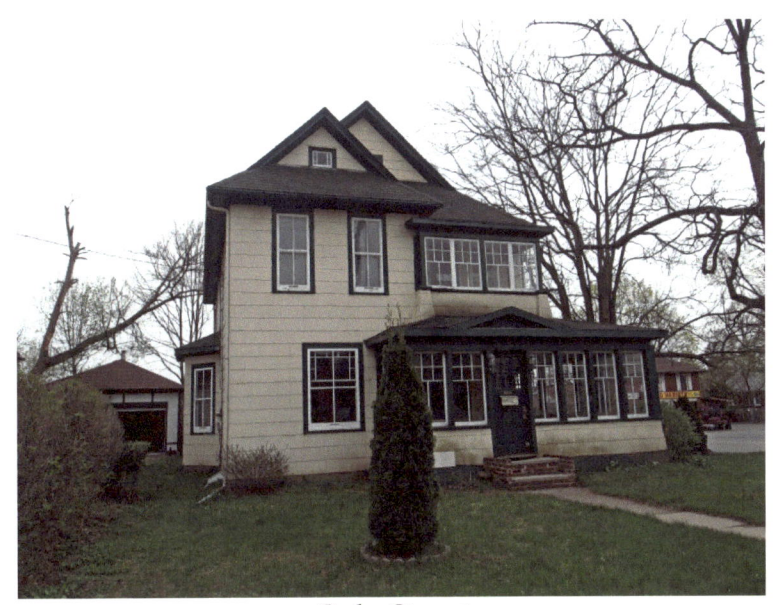

Culp Street

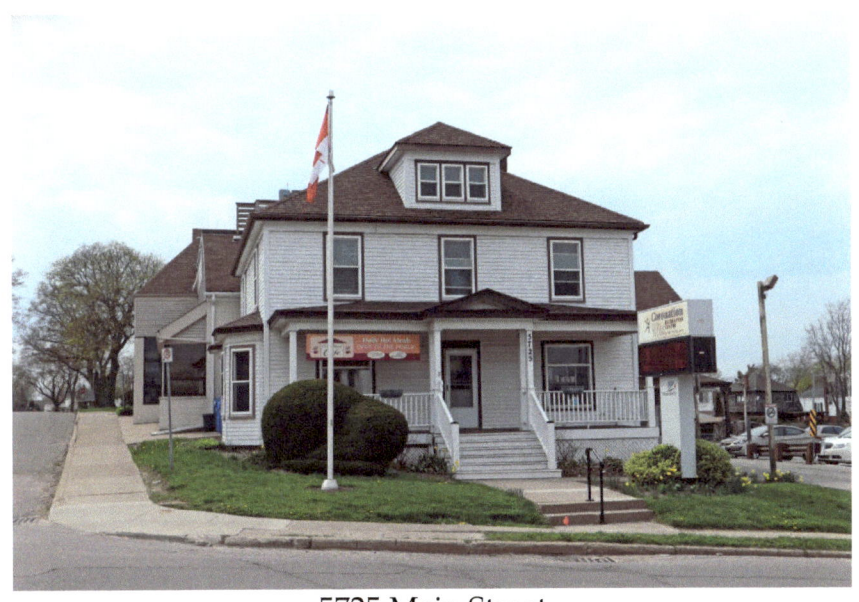

5725 Main Street

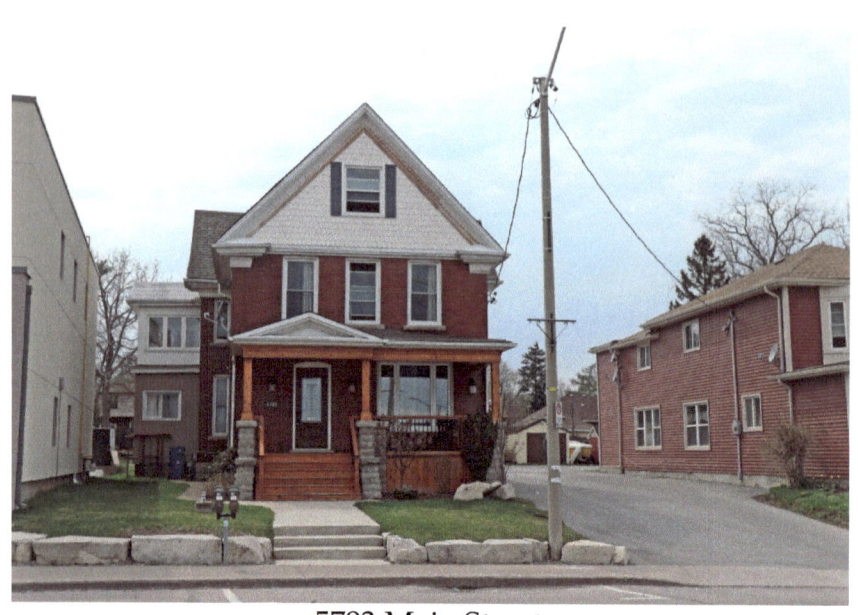

5793 Main Street

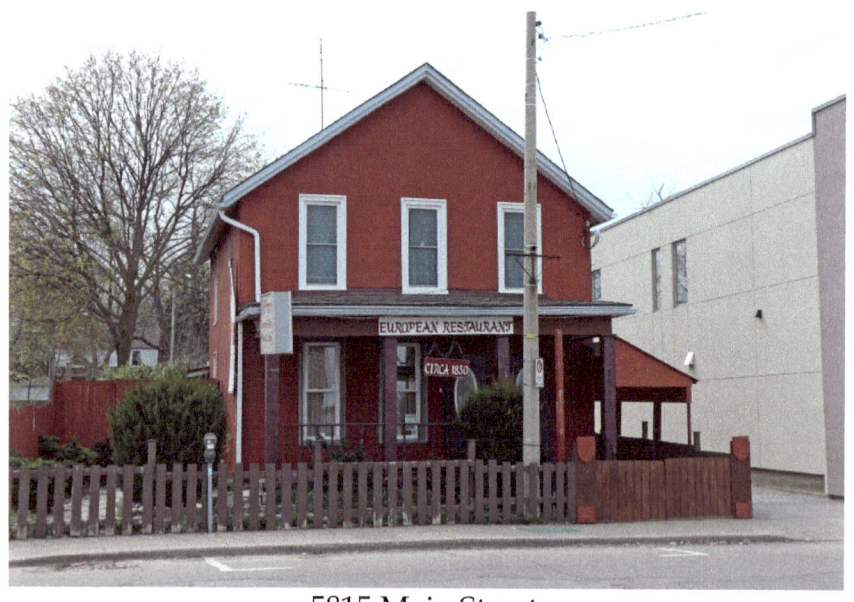

5815 Main Street

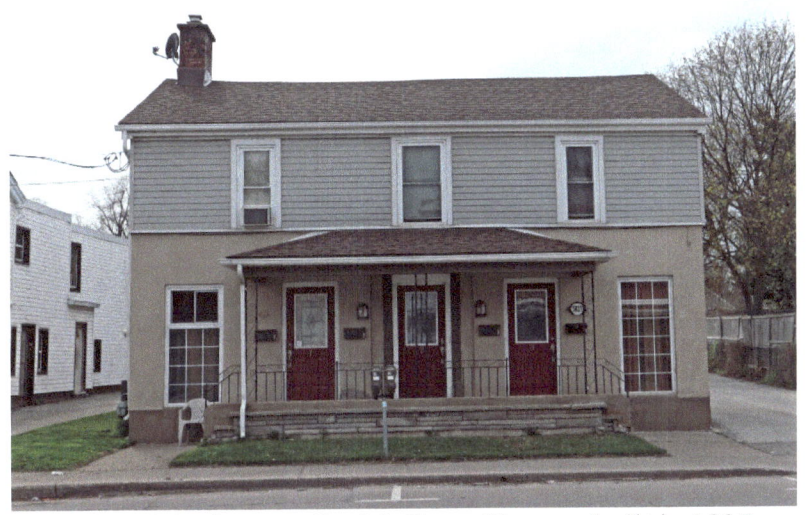

5827 Main Street - Dr. McGarry House – built in 1837

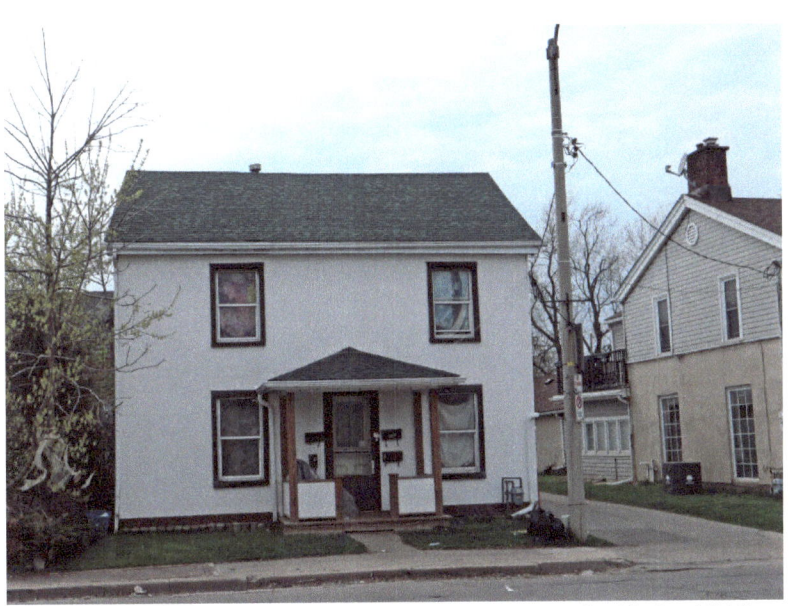

5837 Main Street – The Cole House was built in 1812.

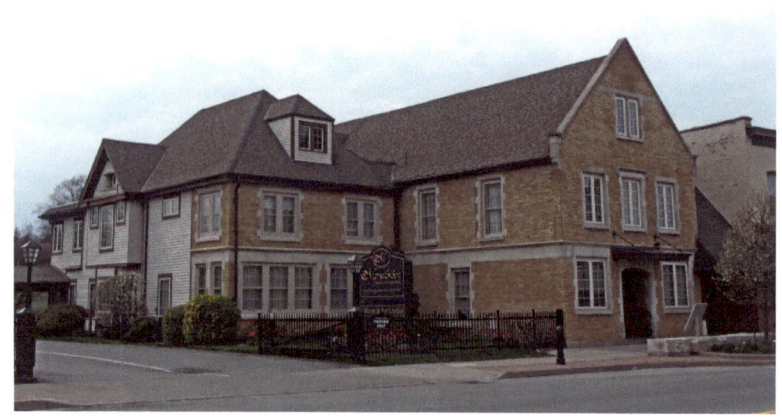

5917 Main Street – Morse & Son Funeral Home

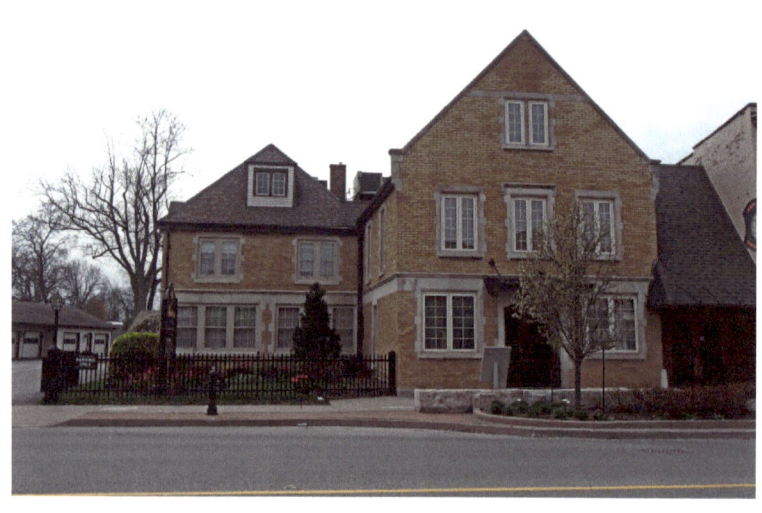

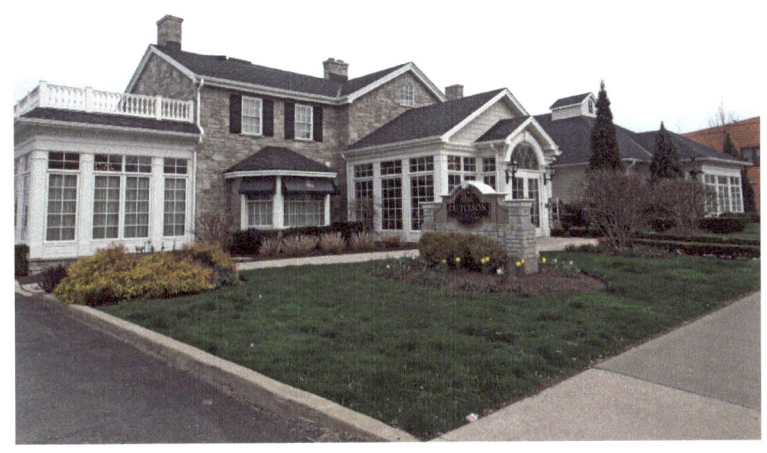

6062 Main Street – Patterson Funeral Home

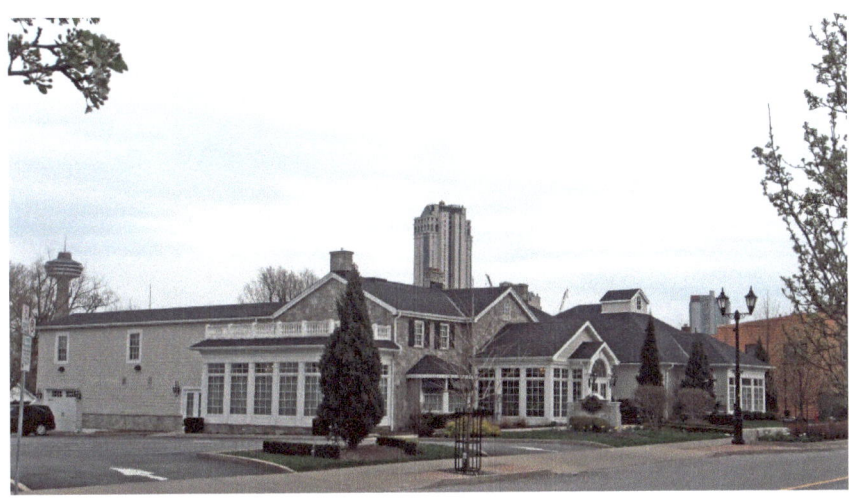

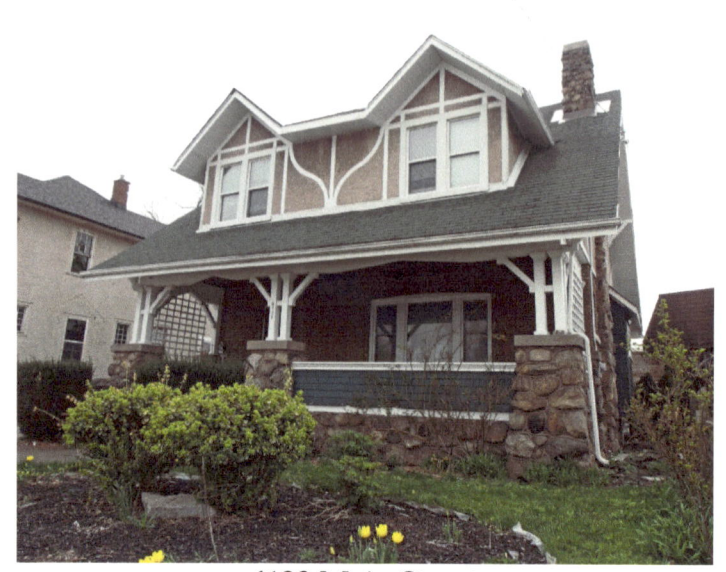

6133 Main Street

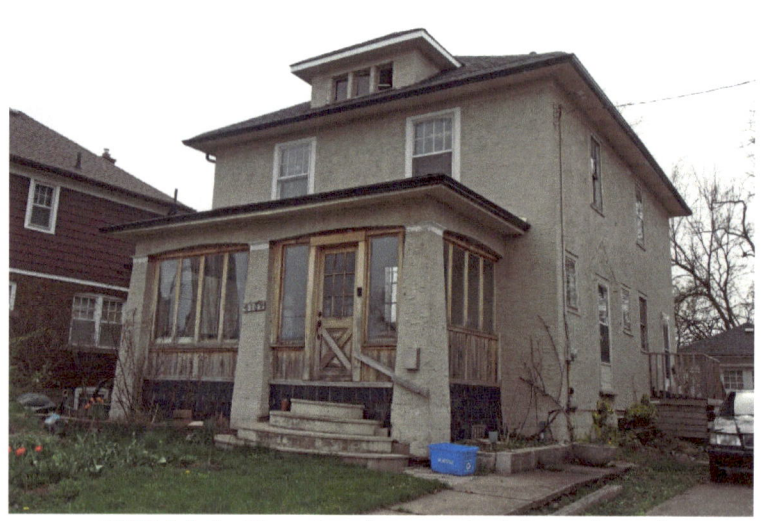

6139 Main Street – dormer in hipped roof

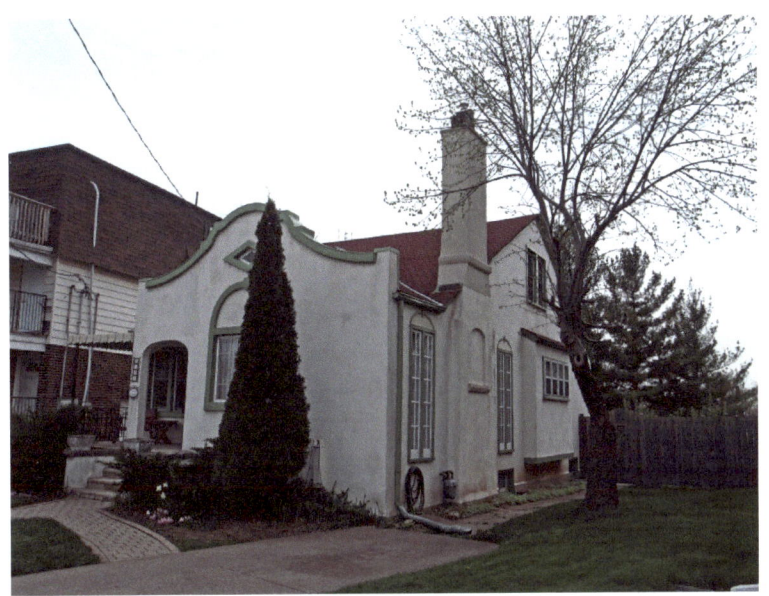

6153 Main Street

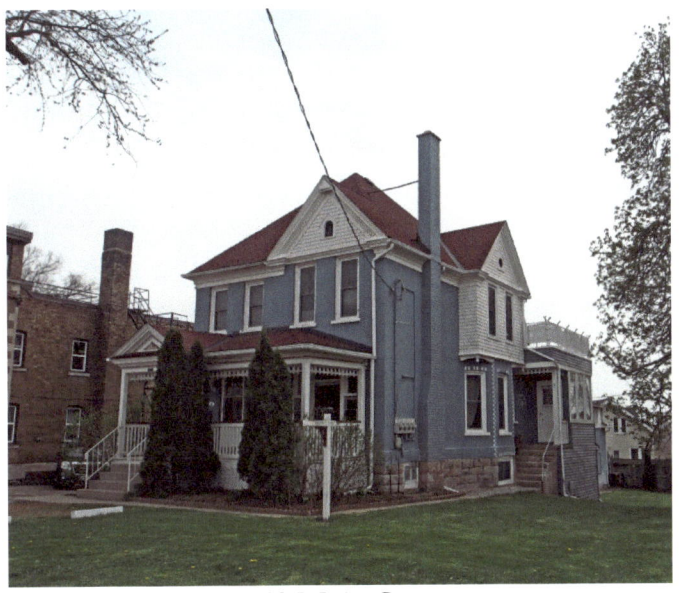

6169 Main Street

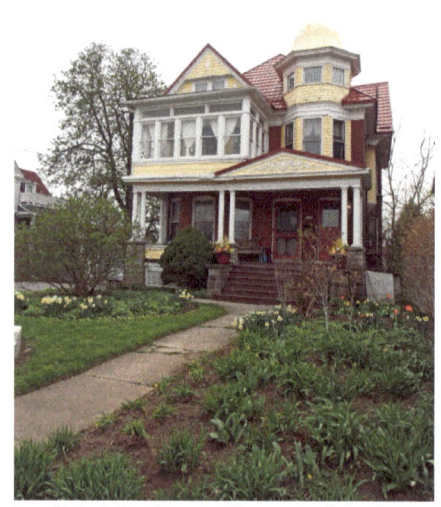

6161 Main Street – "A Night to Remember" Bed & Breakfast - Mary E. Ferguson purchased this lot in 1899 and had this house built for rental purposes. It was built in the Queen Anne Revival style. It has an asymmetrical form with a complex roof. The bay window of the second floor extends to form a third floor tower with a bell-shaped roof. The wraparound porch features columns and a pediment with intricate scroll work.

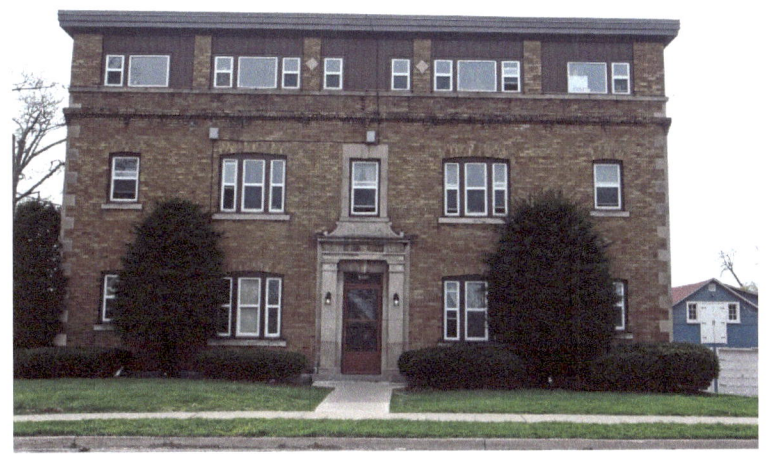

6183 Main Street

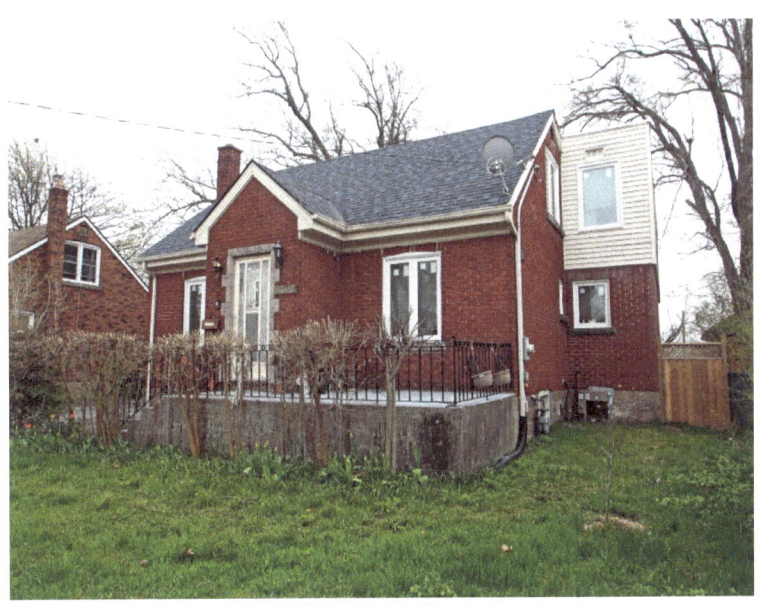

6203 Main Street

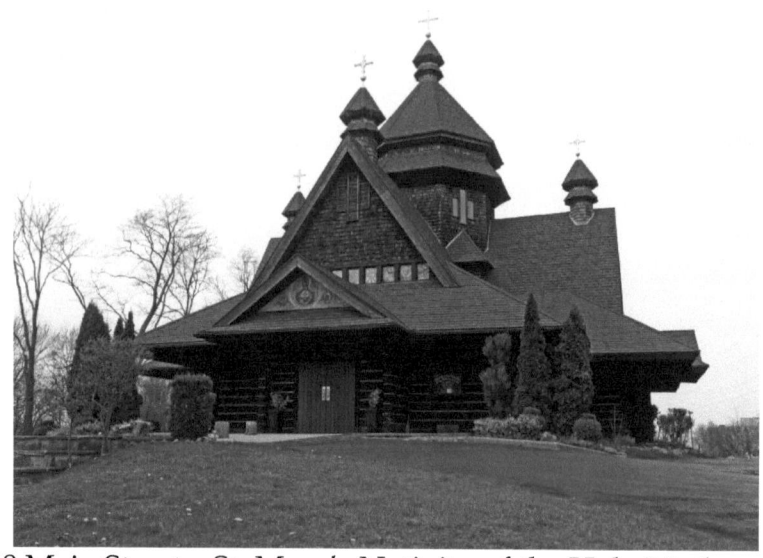

6248 Main Street – St. Mary's Nativity of the Holy Mother of God Ukrainian Catholic Church – It was built by the local congregation to celebrate the 1000th anniversary of the Ukrainian people's conversion to Christianity. The church follows traditional forms of Ukrainian architecture with a central dome over a four-armed cruciform pattern. There are no windows on the lower level as churches were also used as sanctuaries for the villagers when they were attacked by marauding Mongol tribes. St. Mary's was built using huge white pine logs from northern Ontario.

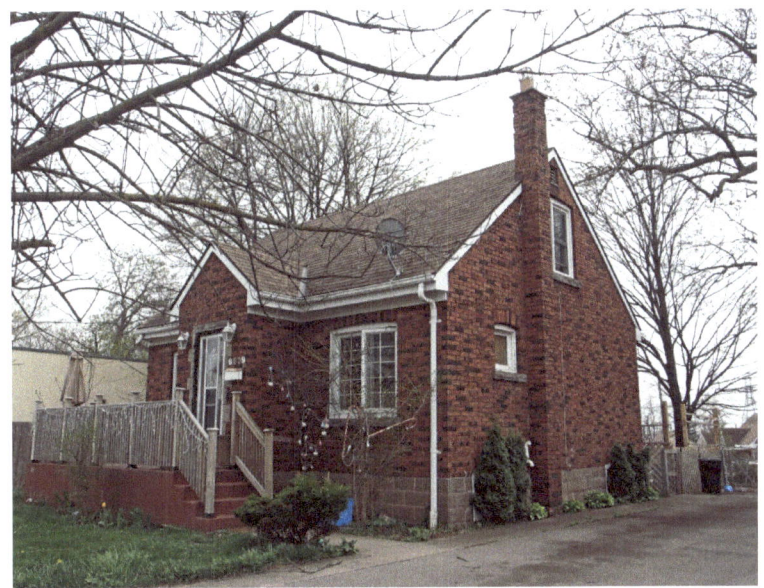

6209 Main Street

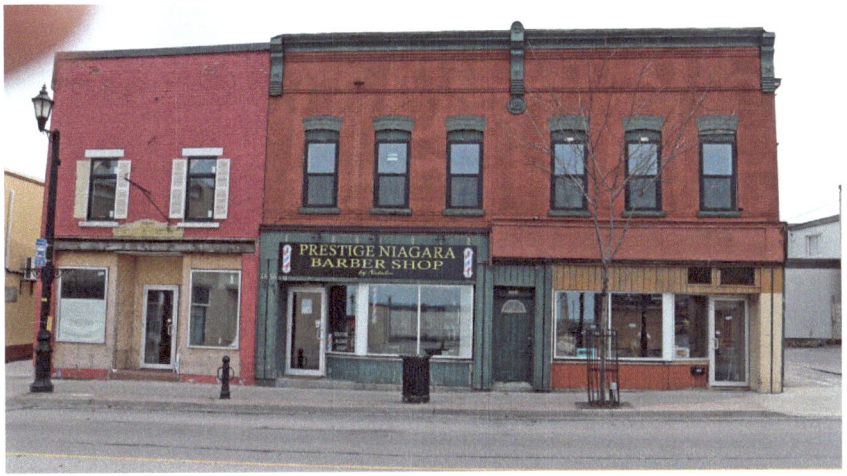

5856 Ferry Street

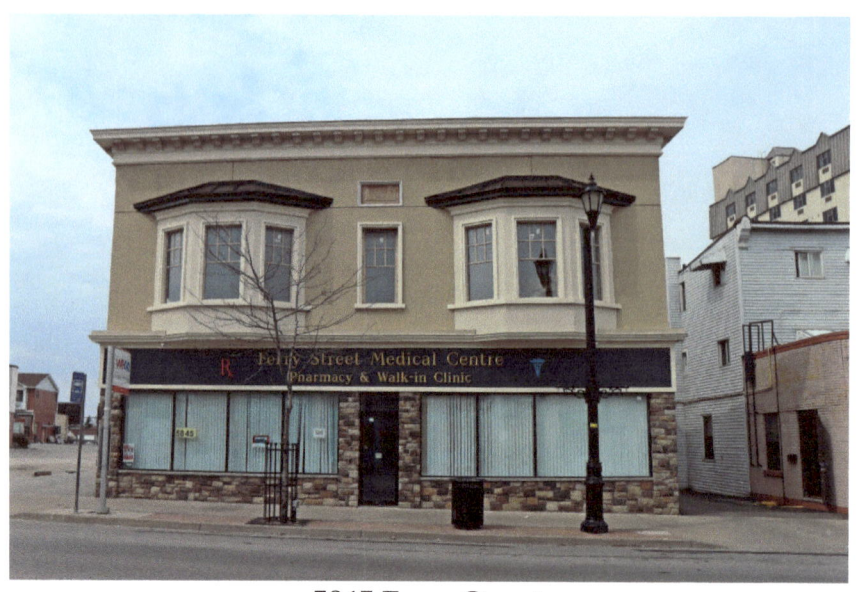

5845 Ferry Street

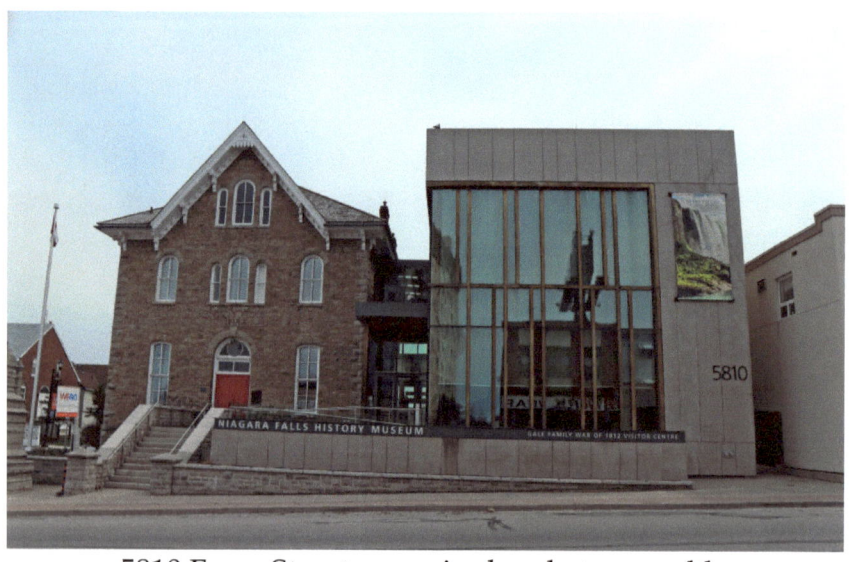

5810 Ferry Street – cornice brackets on gable

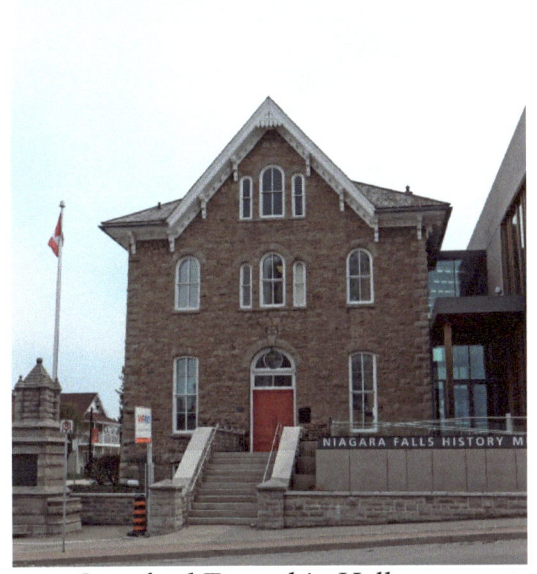

5810 Ferry Street – Stamford Township Hall was erected in 1874. It is now the Niagara Falls History Museum. The hall with its durable hammer dressed limestone construction in its eclectic Italianate styling includes a gabled hip roof with brackets and gingerbread trim, windows of different shape on the first and second stories, and the main entrance archway with a keystone and voussoirs.

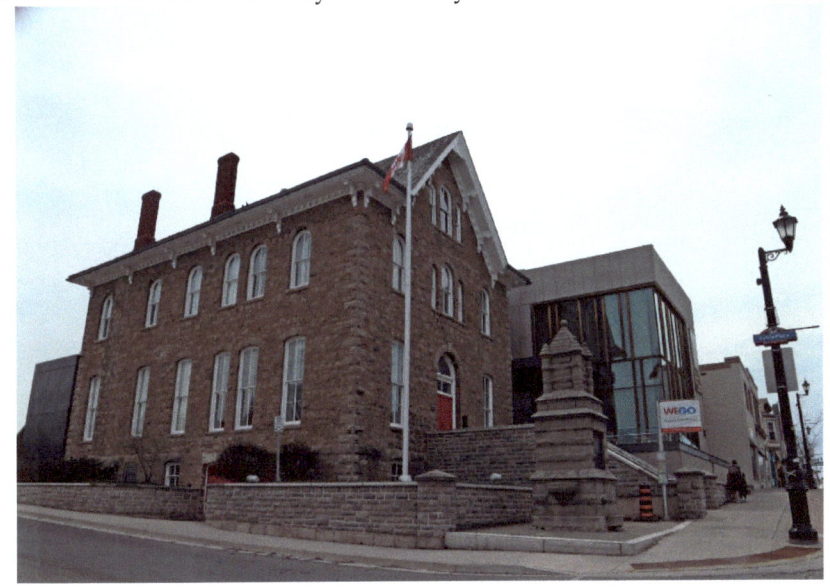

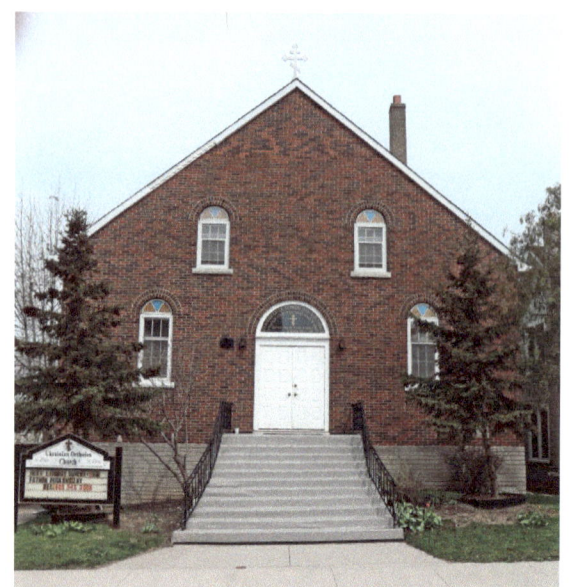

5906 Sylvia Place – Ukrainian Orthodox Church

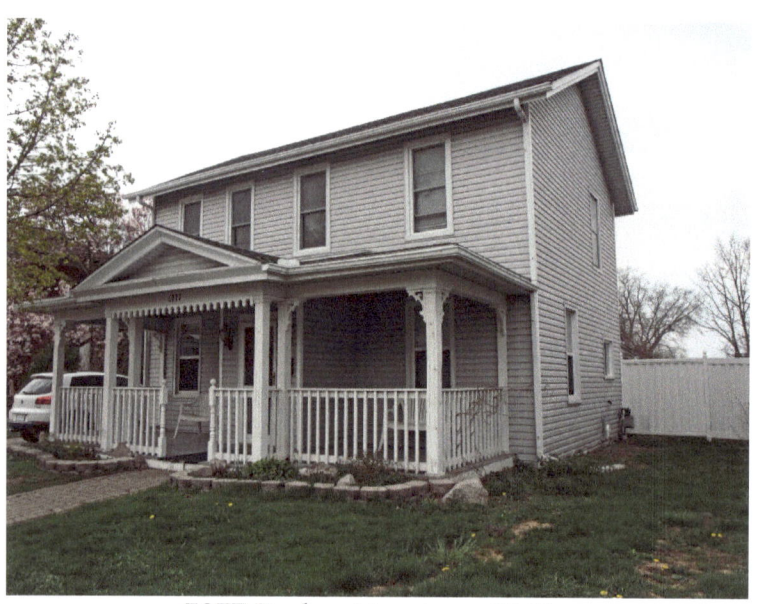

5977 Barker Street – c. 1860s

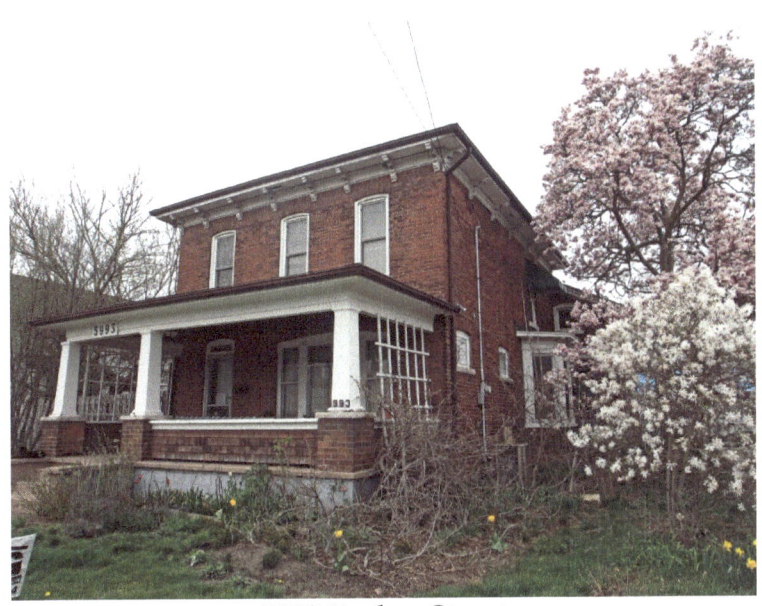

5993 Barker Street

Henry Spence (1809-1894) was a successful mason and builder of the Drummondville area. Born in England, he emigrated to Canada with his family in 1817. He had acquired a significant amount of property over the years in what is now central Drummondville. He also owned a homestead farm on Township Lot 161 south of present day Dunn Street from 1854-1885.

The main part of the house has a square stone foundation; there is a rear wing with a gable roof. There is a semi-elliptical transom over the front door, a large three part parlor window, and a bay window. The front porch with its square tapering support columns is likely an early 20th century addition.

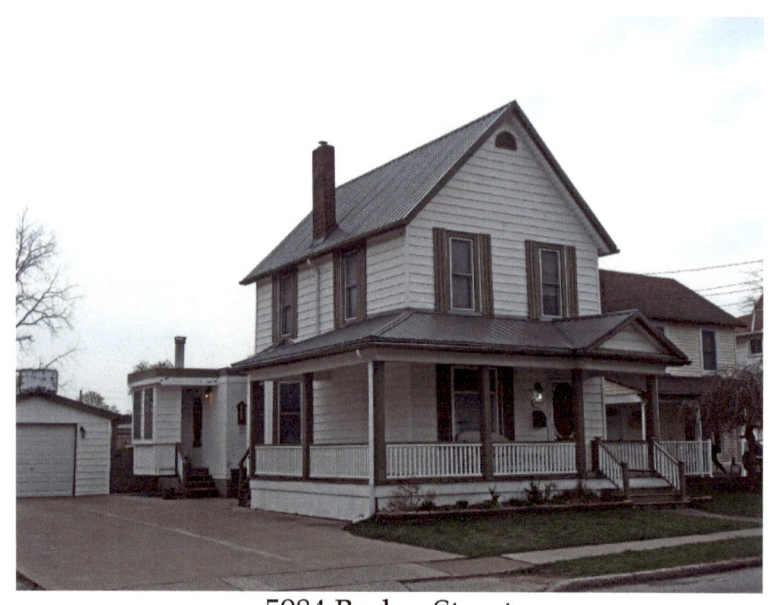
5984 Barker Street

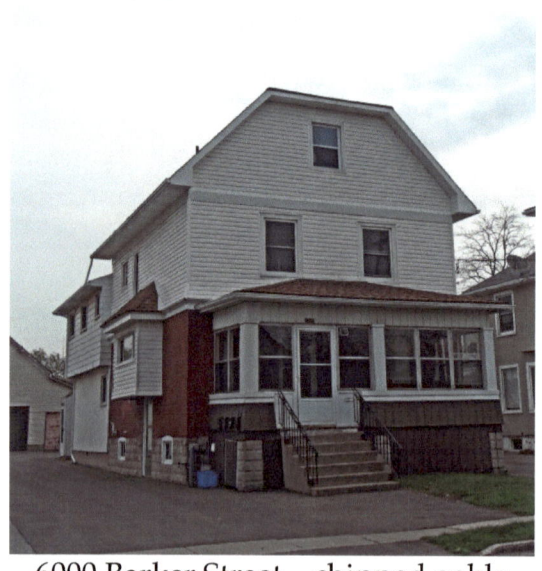
6000 Barker Street – chipped gable

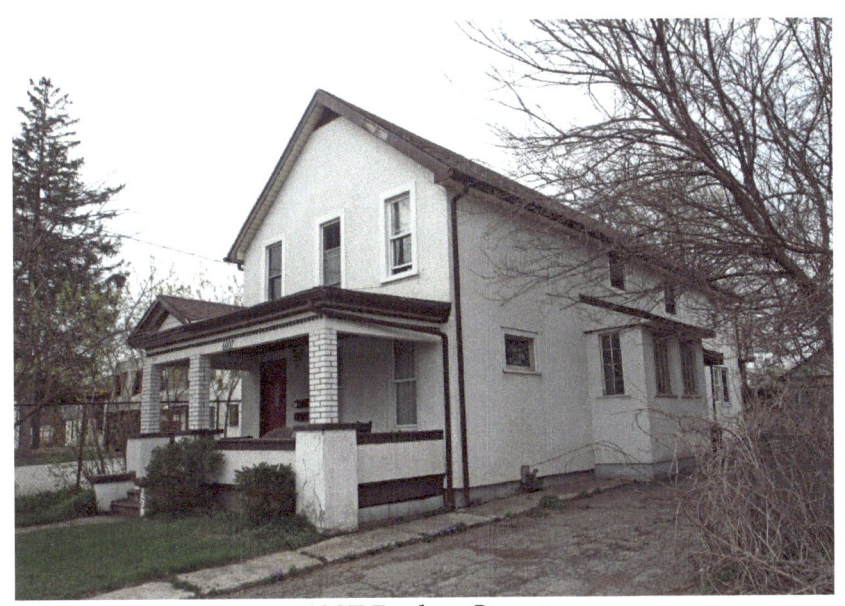

6007 Barker Street

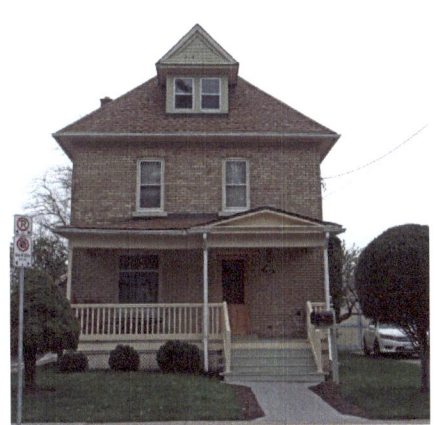

6028 Barker Street

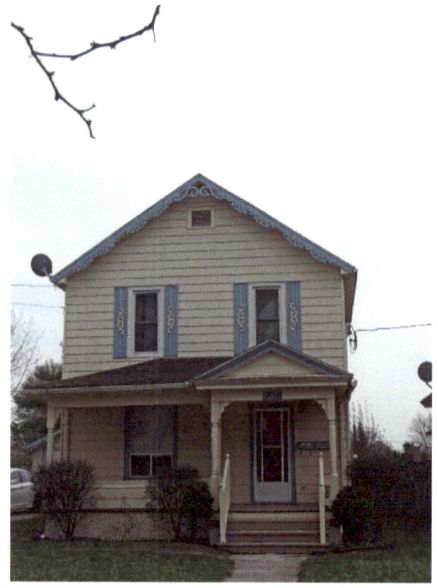
6038 Barker Street

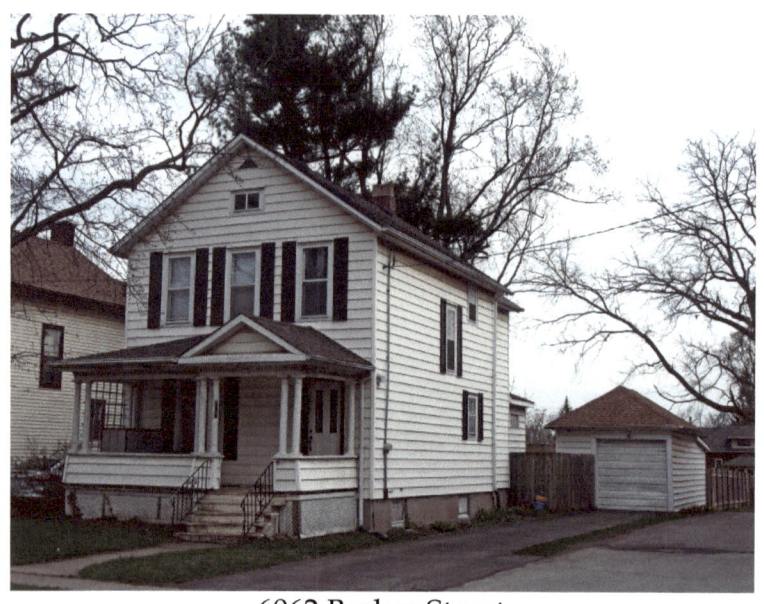
6062 Barker Street

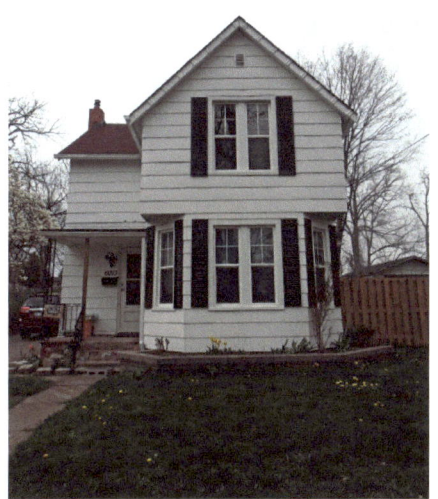

6073 Barker Street

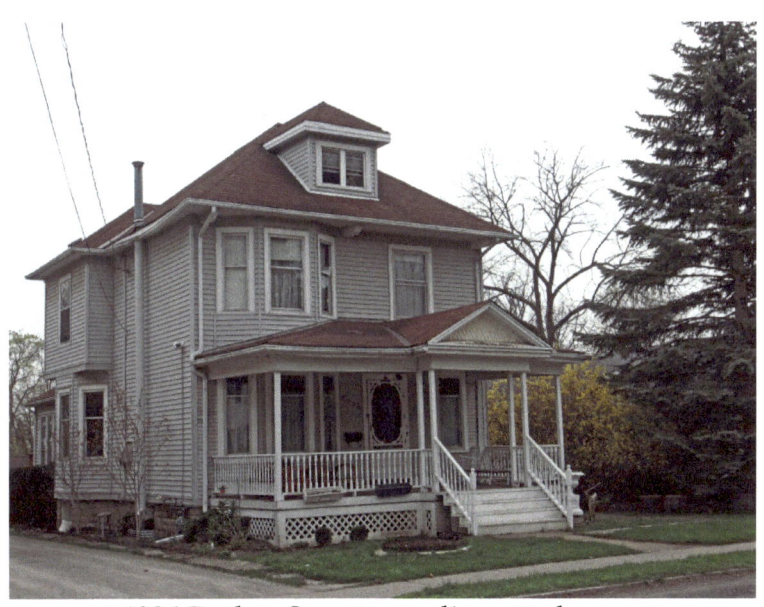

6086 Barker Street – pediment, dormer

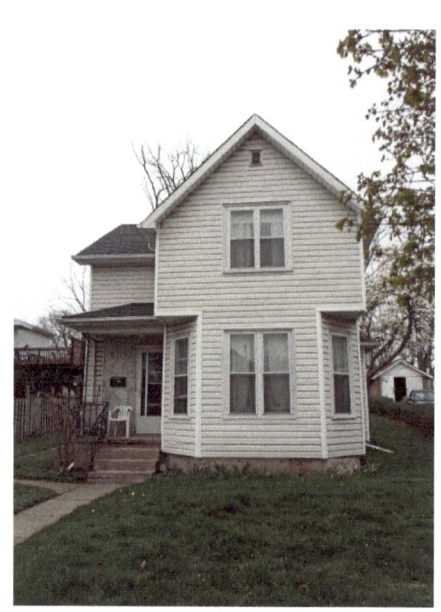

6083 Barker Street

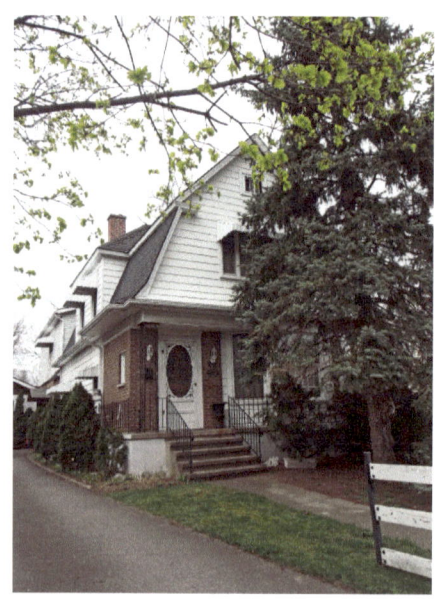

6095 Barker Street – Neo-Colonial – gambrel roof

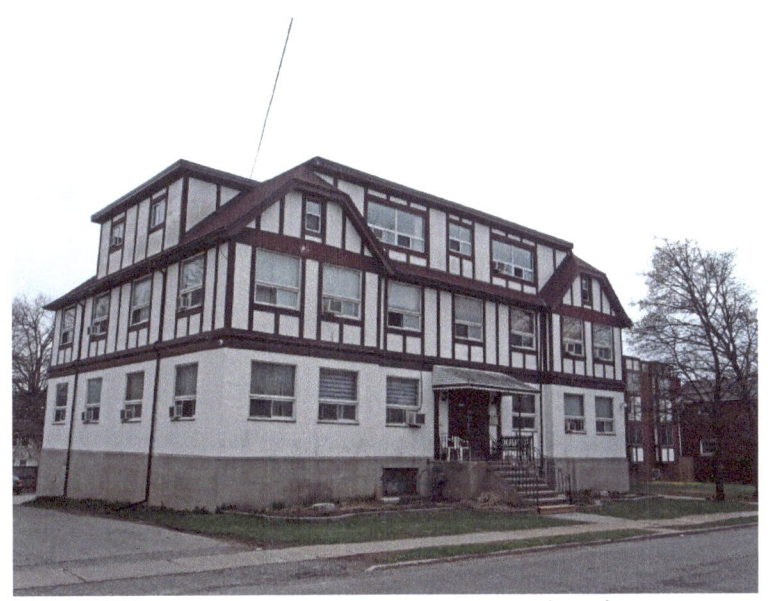

Barker Street – Tudor Revival style

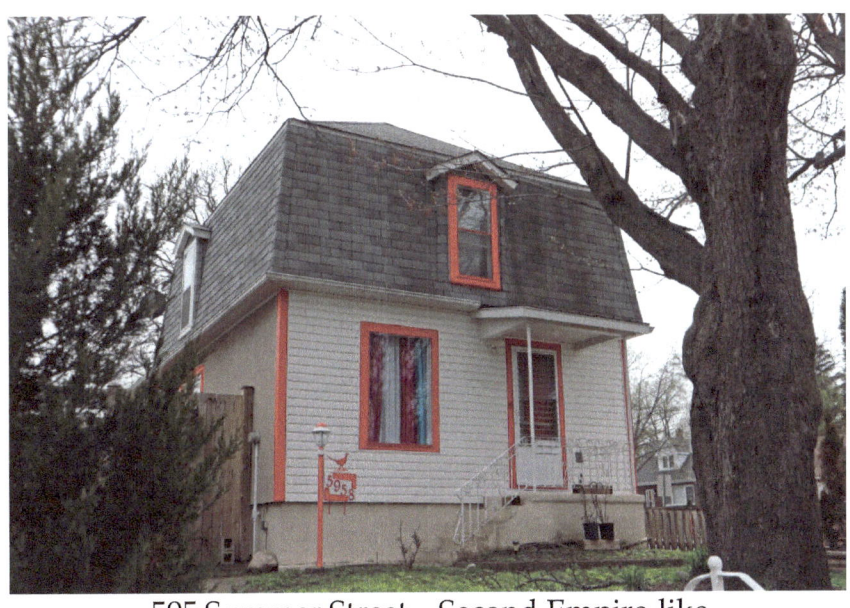

595 Summer Street – Second Empire-like

The Napoleonic Wars raged in Europe from 1803 to 1815. Wishing to remain neutral and to assert its independence, the United States continued to trade with both Britain and France. Nevertheless, diplomatic relations between Britain and the U.S. deteriorated. Forced labor and deplorable conditions on British naval vessels resulted in sailor desertions to the U.S. by the thousands. The U.S. resented the impressment by the British Navy of sailors from American ships. Britain's support of the First Nations in the American northwest threatened U.S. expansion. A persuasive American political faction called the War Hawks emerged who believed victory over British North America would be "a mere matter of marching."

On June 18, 1812, the Americans declared war on Britain. Niagara was a focal point. The British had forts at both ends of the Niagara River (Fort George and Fort Erie) to protect the peninsula from invasion. The major American military base in the area was Fort Niagara.

For three years, Niagara was under almost constant siege. In October of 1812, American forces invaded at Queenston Heights. This was the first major battle between the forces and showed the early weaknesses of the underprepared American Army.

The war resumed in the spring of 1813 with better prepared American forces. An American victory at York (Toronto) encouraged a new Niagara campaign. In May Fort George was captured. They held onto the fort until December 1813 with most of Niagara under American occupation at this time. When the Americans withdrew in December, they burned Niagara-on-the-Lake.

In 1814, the Americans captured Fort Erie and proceeded into the peninsula again with engagements at Chippawa (July 5, 1814), and then Lundy's Lane (July 25, 1814).

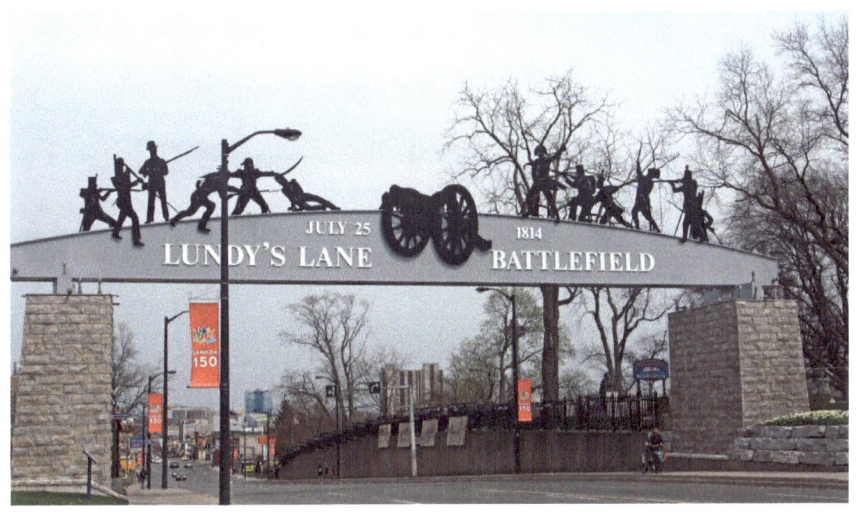

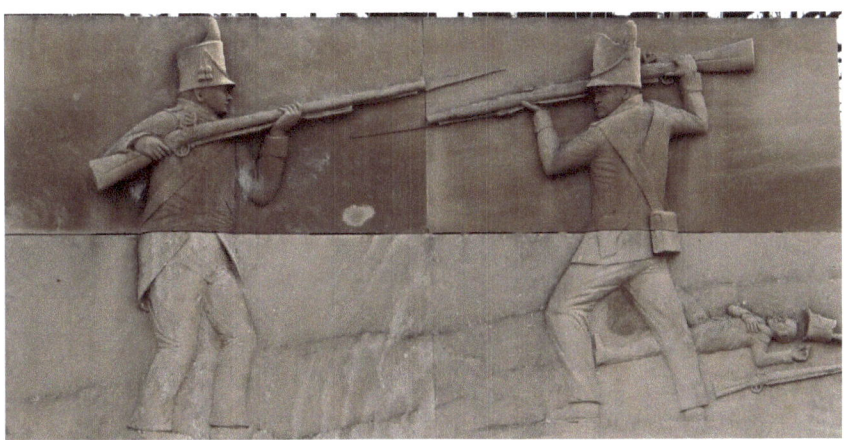

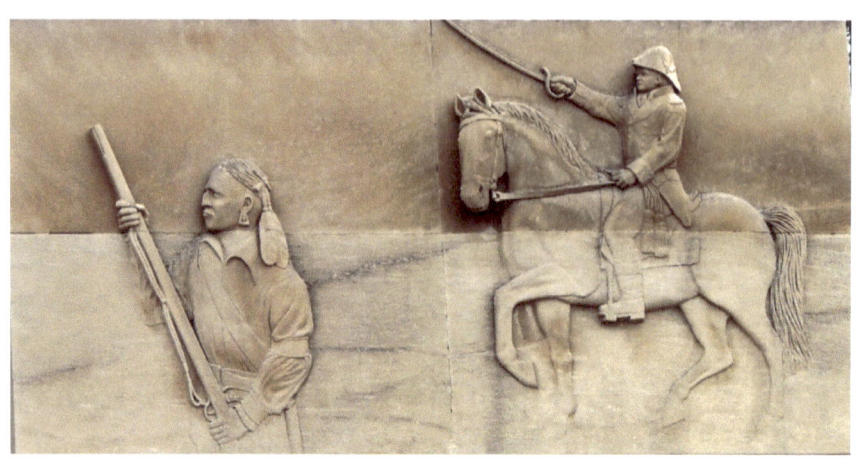

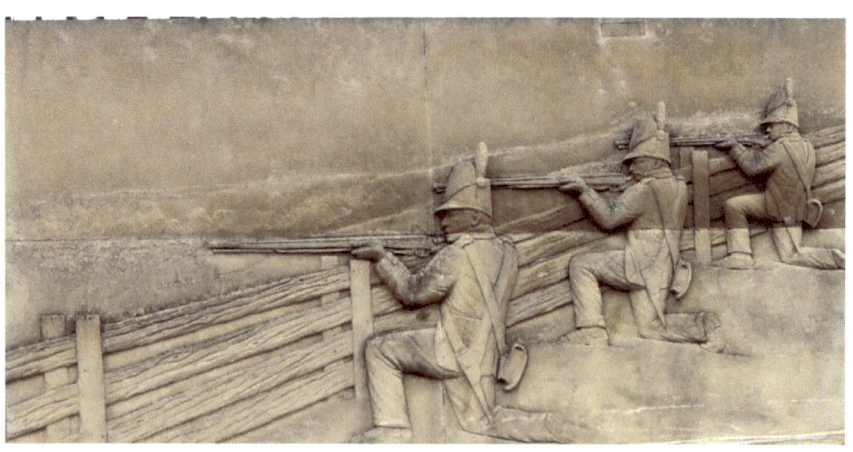

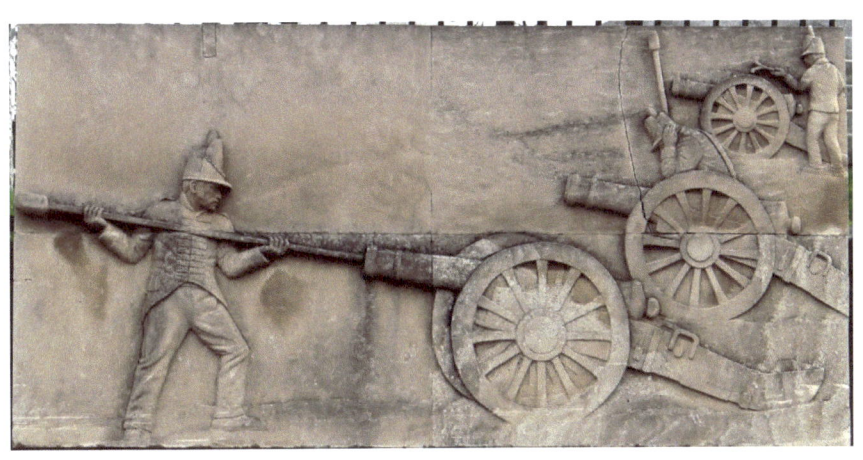

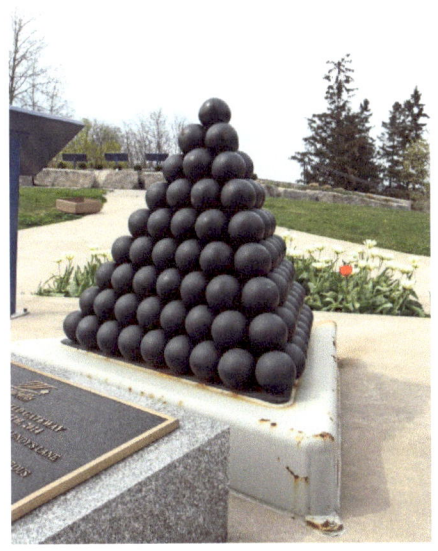

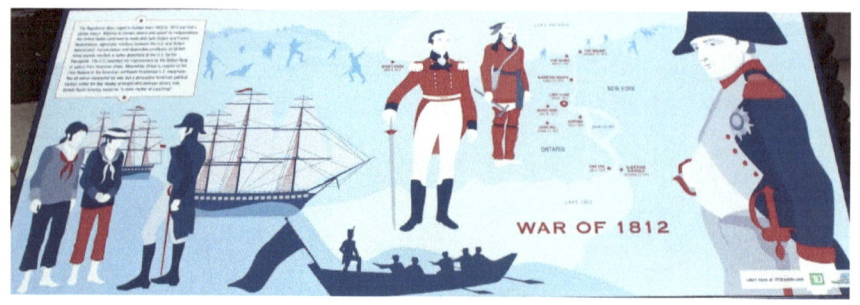

In the early evening of July 25, 1814, the British Commander Lieutenant General Gordon Drummond stood on this hilltop and realized that it would make an excellent defensive position against the advancing American force marching northward in this direction along Portage Road. He set up his artillery pieces (two 24-pounders, two six-pounders and a 5½" howitzer) and deployed his troops (initially 2000 men with later reinforcements of over 1700) in a wide arc to the right and left of the guns.

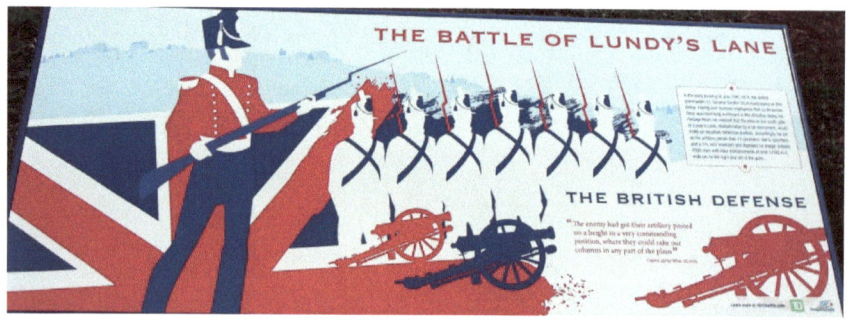

Following the capture of his artillery by the Americans, Lieutenant General Drummond and his troops retreated to the north side of the hill. Drummond led three unsuccessful counterattacks to try and recapture the British guns.

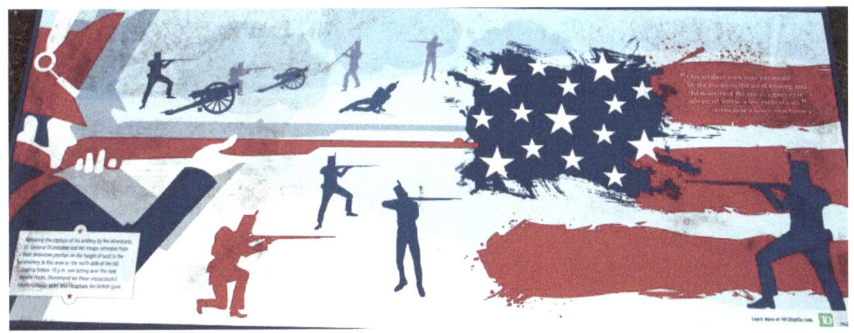

Around midnight, with both sides completely exhausted, the Americans withdrew to their camp at Chippawa. They left the British guns behind, allowing Drummond to reclaim them the following morning.

Following these two clashes, the Americans withdrew to Fort Erie and endured a British siege of the fort (August 15-September 17). In November the American forces retreated across the border and the occupation of the Niagara frontier was over.

The War officially ended on December 24th, 1814 with the signing of the Treaty of Ghent.

Following the close of the War of 1812, because both sides claimed victory here, the battlefield became a popular tourist destination. For many decades, veterans of the battle were available to conduct personal tours.

Adam Fralik, a descendant of a United Empire Loyalist, watched as the tourist industry grew around the War of 1812 battlefield at Lundy's Lane. In 1836, he built the Battle Ground Hotel. The hotel opened as a museum in 2002.

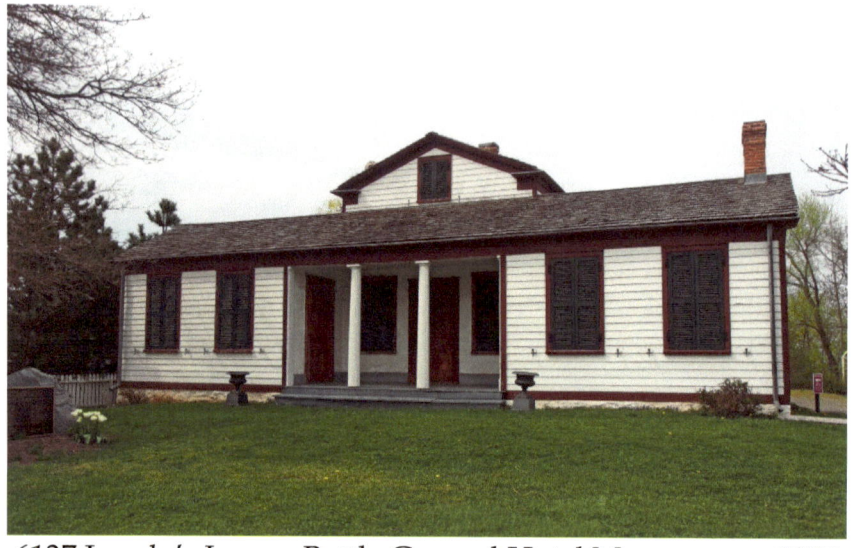

6137 Lundy's Lane – Battle Ground Hotel Museum – c. 1850

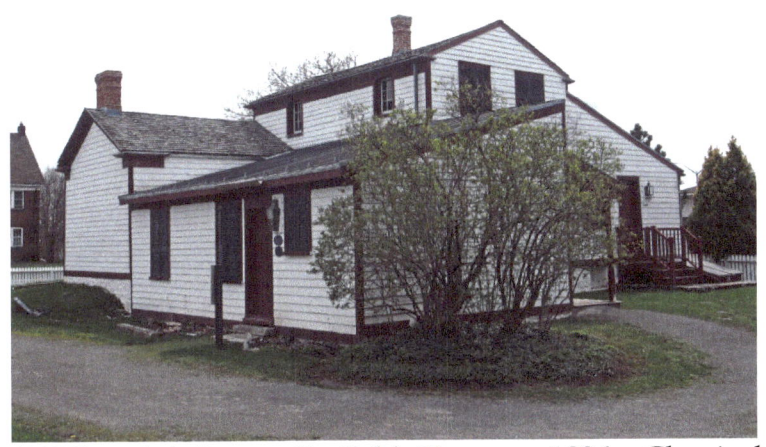

6137 Lundy's Lane – Fralick's Tavern – 1836 – Classical Revival style - The building is symmetrical with a 1½ story section flanked by single story wings.

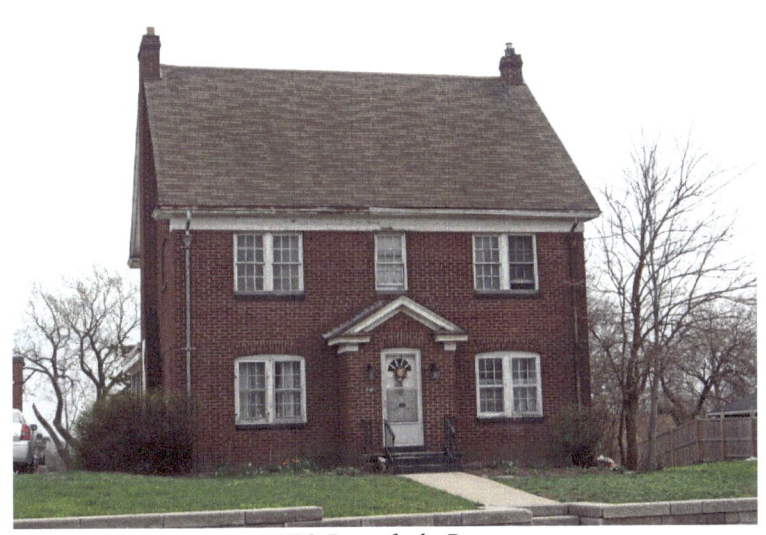

6150 Lundy's Lane

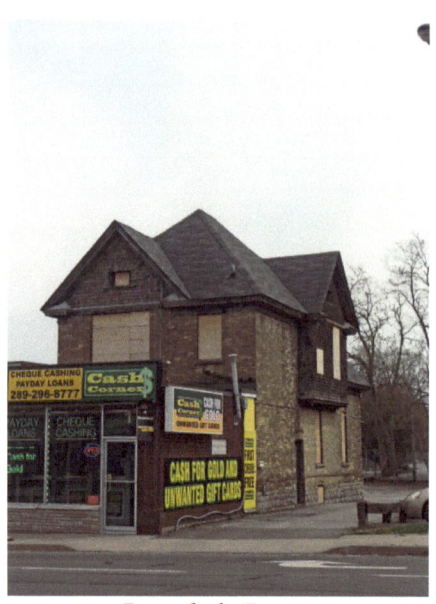

Lundy's Lane

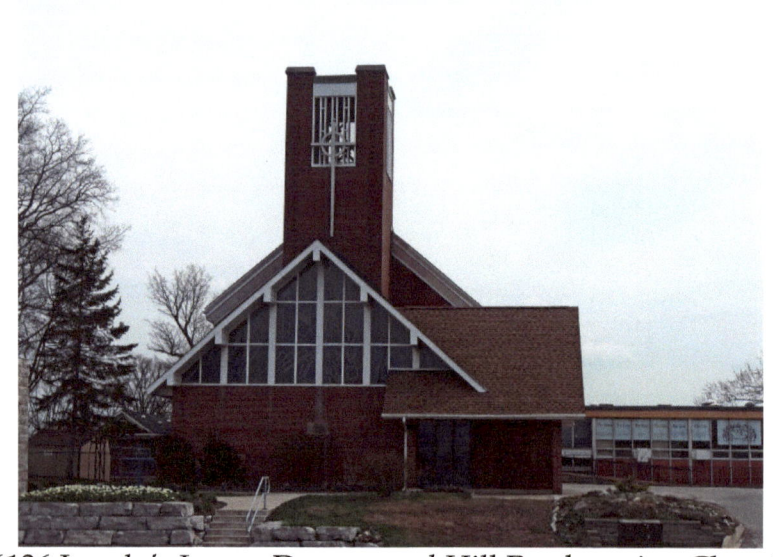

6136 Lundy's Lane - Drummond Hill Presbyterian Church was built 1887-1888

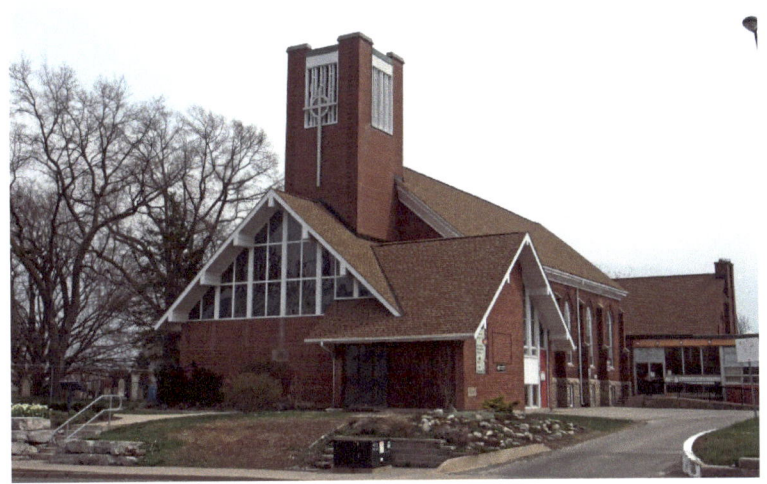

6136 Lundy's Lane

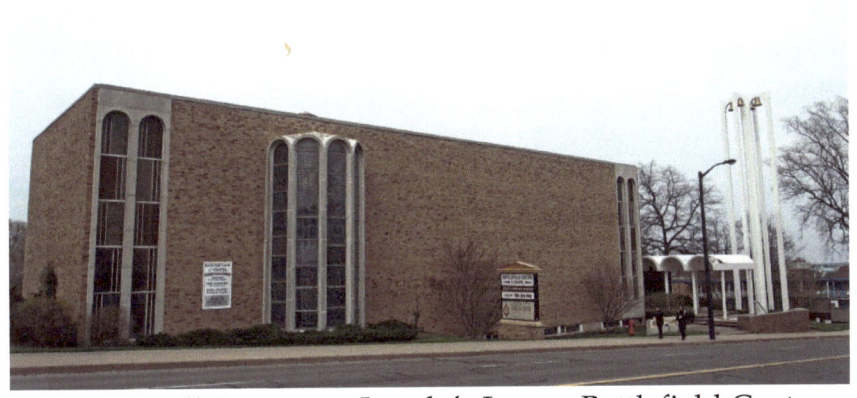

5825 Lowell Avenue at Lundy's Lane – Battlefield Centre Wedding Chapel

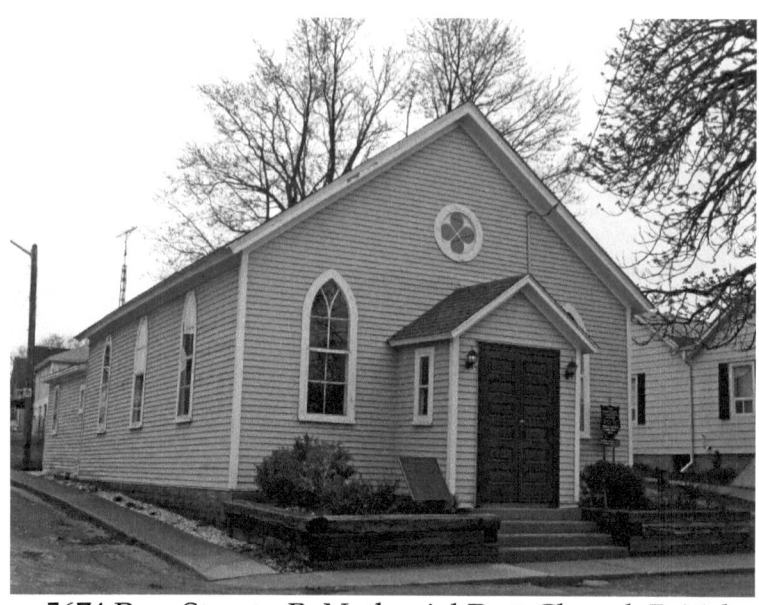

5674 Peer Street - R. Nathaniel Dett Chapel, British Methodist Episcopal Church - The land for the church was donated by Oliver Parnell and his wife Matilda, both of whom had escaped from slavery in the U.S. For many people who followed the Underground Railroad and settled in Niagara Falls, this church served as their spiritual, social and educational center of their community.

The building was moved to its present site in 1856 using logs as rollers. A rear addition was built at the turn of the century as the minister's residence; it is now the Norval Johnson Library. The church was originally covered with clapboard.

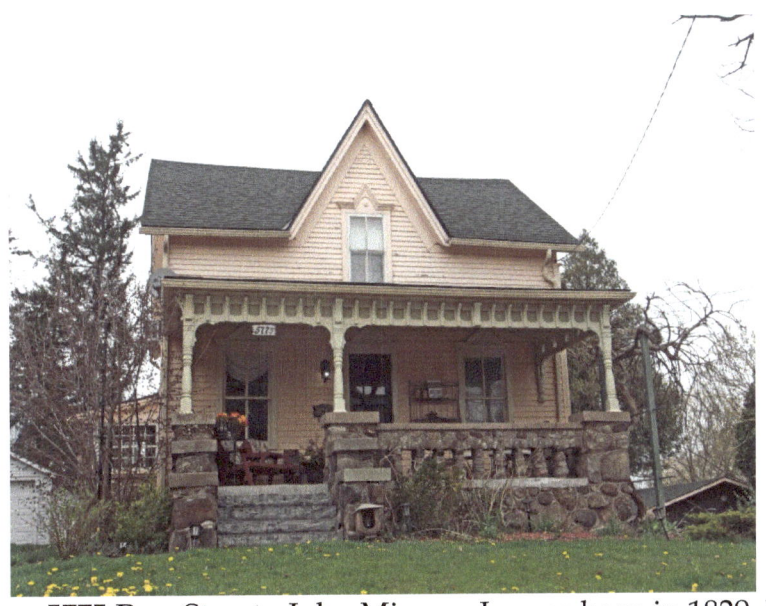

5775 Peer Street - John Misener Jr. was born in 1829. He was 26 when he purchased the land on Peer Street from his father. His father, Captain John Misener owned and operated a wagon-making business on the corner of Main Street and Peer Street. John Misener Jr. assumed the wagon-making business after his father's death in 1855.

The house, c. 1855, is in the Ontario Gothic style with a central gable in the roof. The gable window design with a pediment is an adaptation of Italianate form. The field stone wall of the verandah was a later addition. The upper portion of the verandah features elaborate woodwork with turned posts.

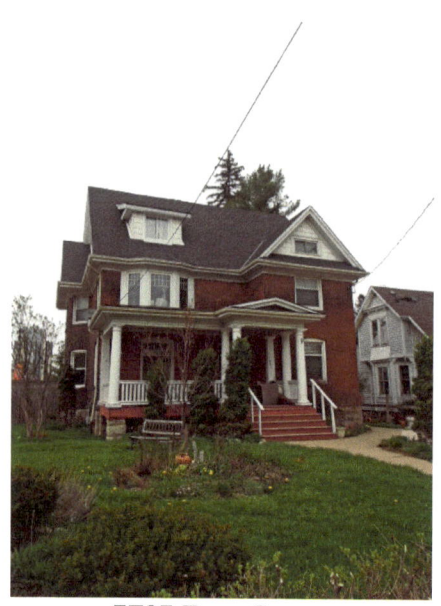

5795 Peer Street

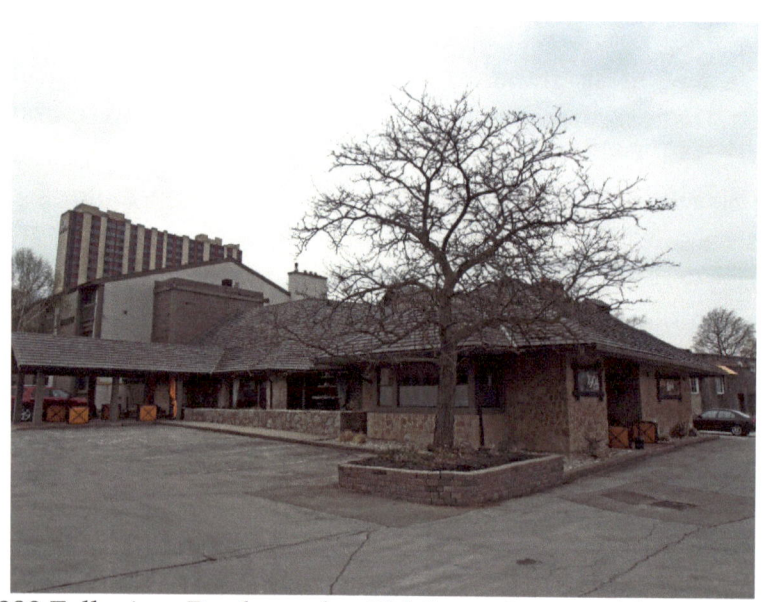

6080 Fallsview Boulevard – Old Stone Inn established 1904

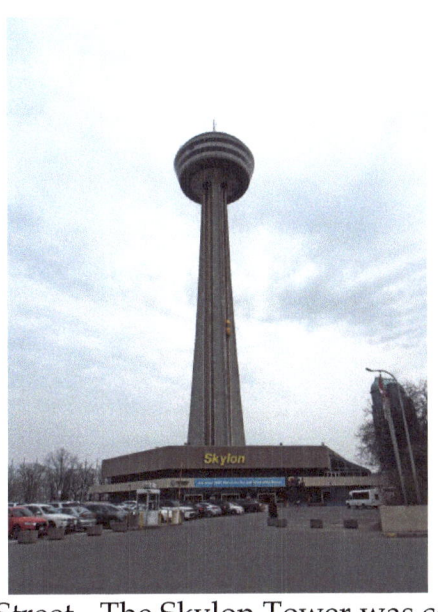

5200 Robinson Street - The Skylon Tower was constructed in 1964-65 and is an observation tower that overlooks both the American Falls, New York and the larger Horseshoe Falls, Ontario, from the Canadian side of the Niagara River. It is 160 meters (520 feet) tall from street level. The tower has three outside mounted "Yellow Bug" elevators and can carry passengers to the top of the tower in 52 seconds. The tower has two restaurants at its top, the lower Revolving Dining Room and the upper Summit Suite Buffet. The Revolving Dining Room seats 276 people and revolves once every hour. An observation deck is at the tower's summit. The base of the tower features gift shops, fast food restaurants and a large amusement arcade.

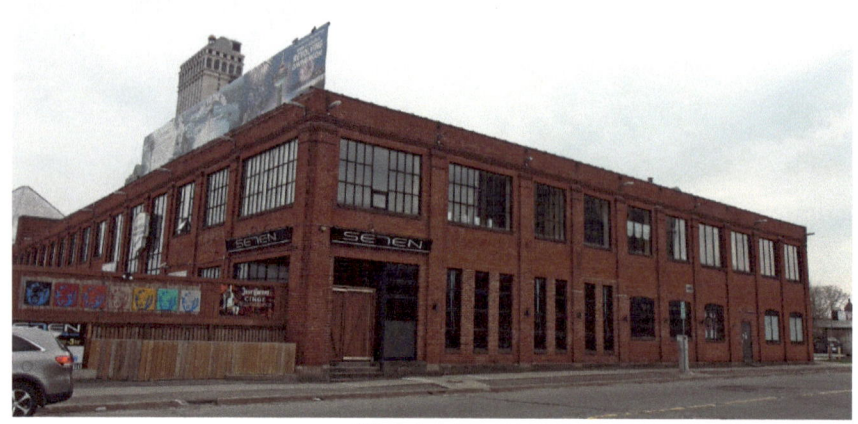

Old factory

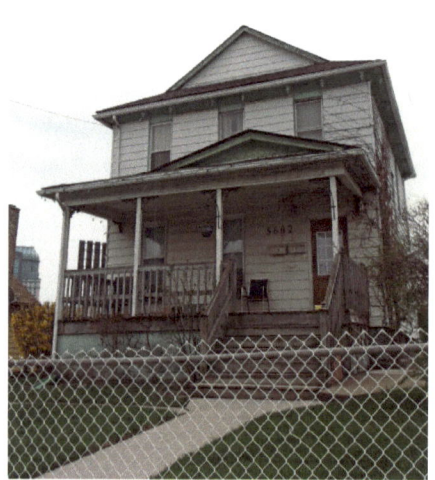

5602 Robinson Street

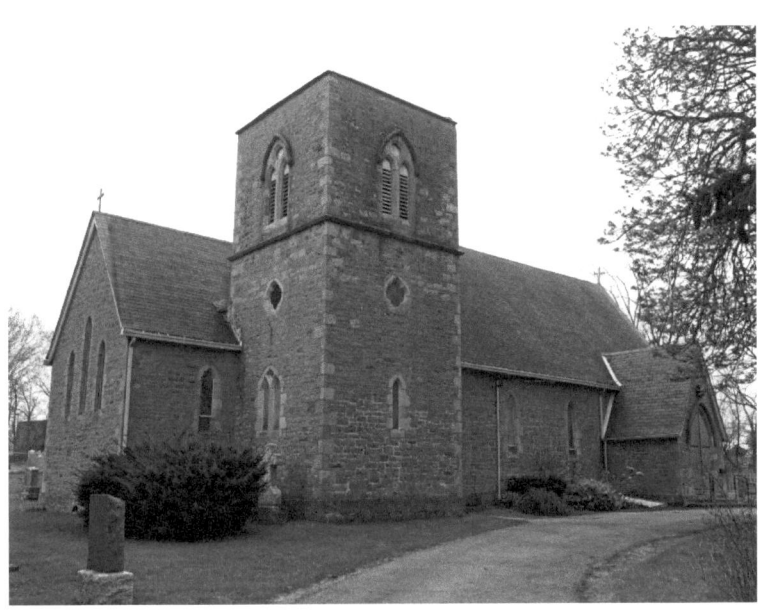

Robinson Street – old church

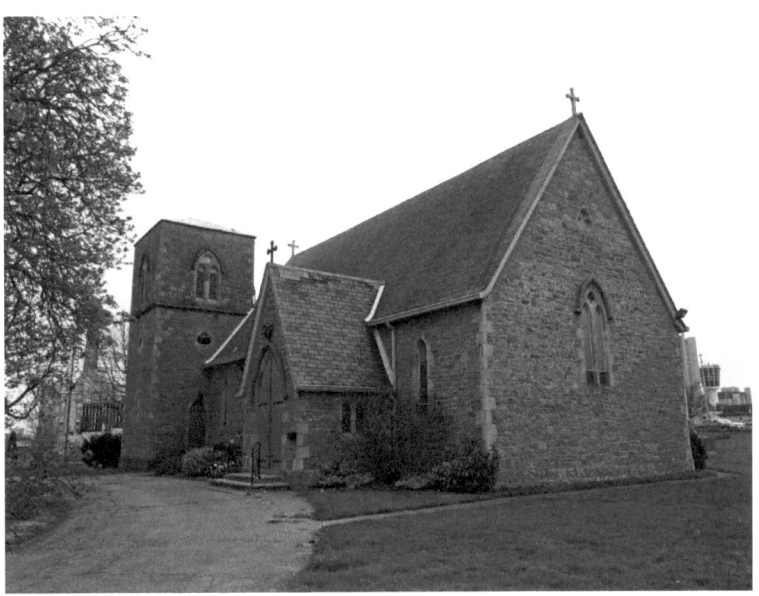

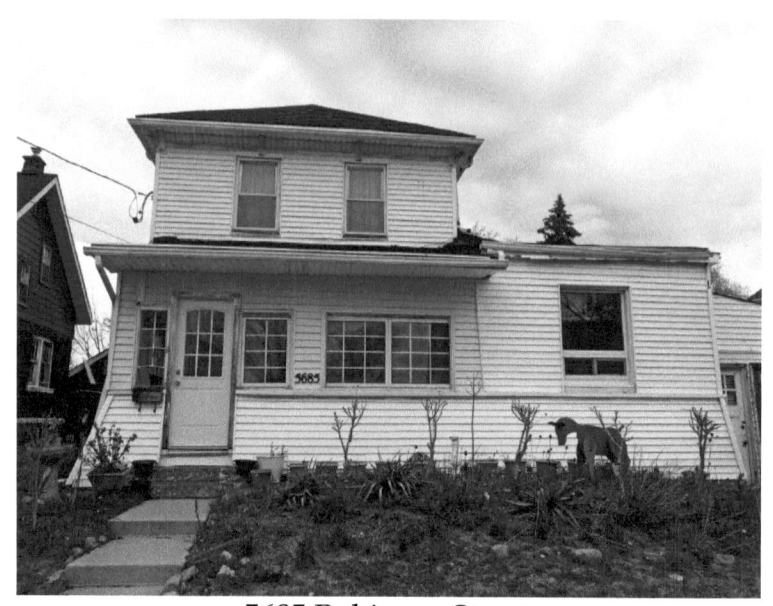

5685 Robinson Street

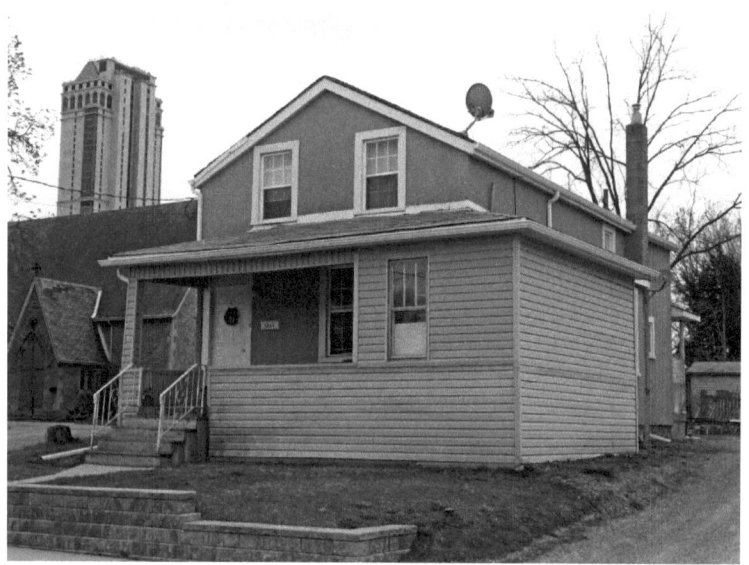

5688 Robinson Street

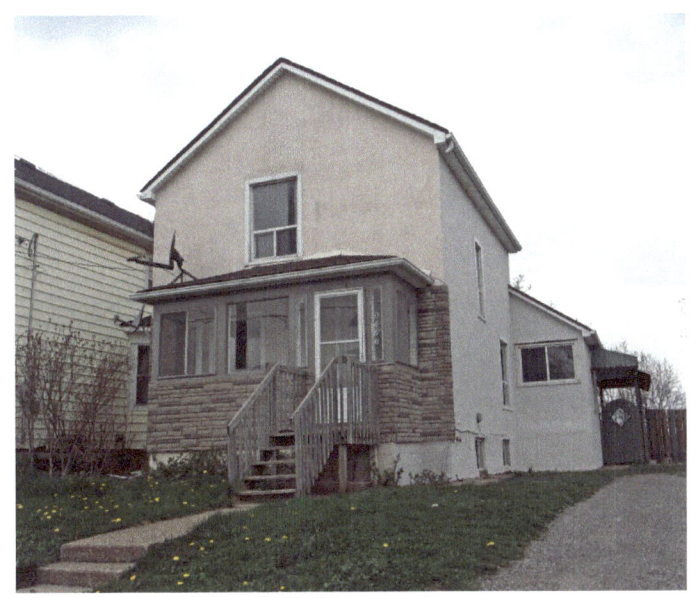

5777 Robinson Street

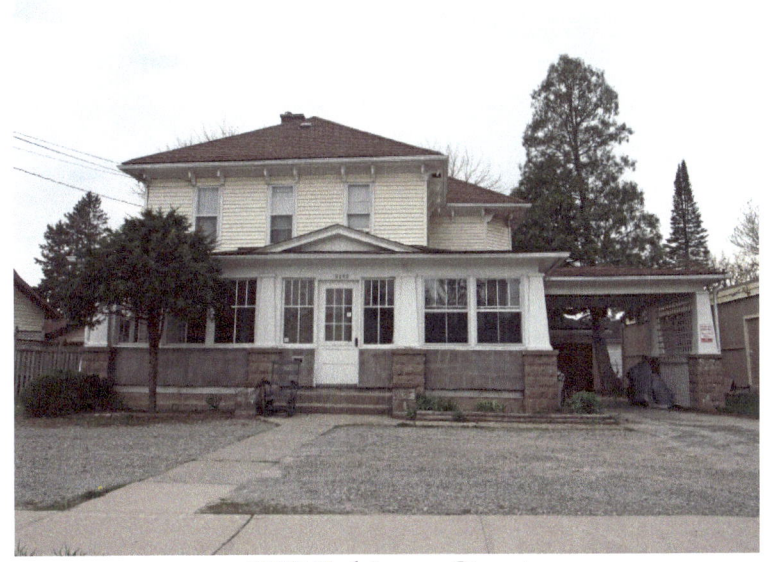

6395 Robinson Street

Building Styles

Arts and Crafts: The overlying theme - the house was based on the function of the house. Rooms were oriented to take advantage of the movement of the sun for warmth and light during daylight hours. Side entrances allowed for useable space on the front facade for light or garden use. Features include: wood, stone or stucco siding; low-pitched roof; wide eaves with triangular brackets; exposed roof rafters; porch with thick square or round columns; stone porch supports; exterior chimney made with stone; open floor plans with few hallways; many windows, some with stained or leaded glass; beamed ceilings; dark wood wainscoting and moldings; built-in cabinets, shelves, and seating.

Edwardian, 1900-1930 – This style bridges the ornate and elaborate styles of the Victorian era and the simplified styles of the 20th century. Edwardian Classicism provided simple, balanced facades, simple rooflines, dormer windows, large front porches, and smooth brick surfaces. Voussoirs and keystones are used sparingly and are understated. Finials and cresting are absent. Cornice brackets and braces are block-like and openings have flat arches or plain stone lintels.

Gothic Revival, 1830-1890 – These decorative buildings have sharply-pitched gables with highly detailed verge boards, pointed-arch window openings, and dichromatic brickwork. It is a common style in Ontario.

Italianate, 1850-1900 – A two story rectangular building with a mild hip roof, a projecting frontispiece, and generous eaves with ornate cornice brackets was the basis of the style; often there are large sash windows, quoins, ornate detailing on the windows, belvederes and wraparound verandahs. Italianate commercial buildings often have cast iron cresting and elegant window surrounds.

Neo-Colonial (also Colonial Revival, Georgian Revival or Neo-Georgian) architecture seeks to revive elements of architectural style of American colonial architecture of the period around the Revolutionary War which drew strongly from Georgian architecture of Great Britain. Architecture from the 18th and early 19th centuries in Ontario includes a wide assortment of detailing and ornament applied to a design centered around the fireplace and the source of water. Structures are typically two stories, have a symmetrical front facade with elaborate front doorways, often with decorative crown pediments, fanlights, and sidelights, symmetrical windows flanking the front entrance, often in pairs or threes, and columned porches.

Ontario Cottage - one or one-and-a-half story buildings with a cottage or hip roof. The cottage roof is an equal hip roof where each hip extends to a point in the center of the roof. The hip roof has a long hip in the center. The Ontario Cottage is the vernacular design of the Regency Cottage which generally has a more ornate doorway and a partial or full verandah surrounding it. The roof can have a dormer, a belvedere, and generally two chimneys.

Queen Anne, 1885-1900 – This style is distinguished by an irregular outline featuring a combination of an offset tower, broad gables, projecting two-story bays, verandahs, multi-sloped roofs, and tall, decorative chimneys. A mixture of brick and wood is common. Windows often have one large single-paned bottom sash and small panes in the upper sash.

Regency Cottage, 1830-1860 – This style originated in England in 1815 and spread to Ontario later in the 19th century as British officers retired to Canada. It is a modest one-story house with a low-pitched hip roof and has a symmetrical front façade.

The **Stick Style,** 1860-1890 - is named after its use of linear "stickwork" (overlay board strips) on the outside walls to mimic an exposed half-timbered frame. Stick style houses are almost always made with wood. It has a plain layout, often accented with trusses on the gables or decorative shingles. Other characteristics include interpenetrating roof planes with bold paneled brick chimneys, wraparound porch, spindle detailing, the "paneled" sectioning of blank wall, and radiating spindle details at the gable peaks.

Tudor Revival – exposed timbers with stucco infill, multi-paned windows.

Other Books by Barbara Raue

Coins of Gold
Arrows, Indians and Love
The Life and Times of Barbara
The Cromwell Family Book
Laura Secord Discovered
Daddy Where Are You?

Montana Series
Book 1: Montana Dream
Book 2: Life on the Montana Frontier
Book 3: Montana to Boston and Back
Book 4: Montana Sons Go to War
Book 5: Montana Sons Return from War

Donaldson Series
Book 1: Rite of Passage
Book 2: Rite of Marriage

© 2021 by Barbara Raue - All the photos in this book have been taken with my cameras. I own the rights to them.

Barbara is The Authority on Saving Our History One Photo at a Time. She is pursuing her interest in photography and architecture by preserving a record through photos of old buildings from the 1800s and 1900s with their unique architecture. Enjoy the beautiful architecture in the comfort of your living room. Dream about what it was like in those by-gone days. Dream about what it was like to live in a mansion like one of those in this book.

Barbara Raue, a wife, mother and grandmother, is an avid reader and writer. She has researched and compiled several family histories. In 2010, Barbara published her book "Coins of Gold," which celebrates the courageous life of her mother, May Todd. Barbara's second book is a historical fiction "Arrows, Indians and Love" which takes place in Boonesborough, Kentucky during the time of Daniel Boone. In 2013, Barbara published *The Cromwell Family Book* in which she traces her ancestry generations back into Great Britain. Her second novel is called *Laura Secord Discovered,* in which the story of Laura's service during the War of 1812 is shared. Barbara's memoir is titled *Daddy Where Are You?* It tells of her life growing up without a father. Five novels in the Montana Series have been published, *Montana Dream, Life on the Montana Frontier, Montana to Boston and Back, Montana Sons Go to War,* and *Montana Sons Return from War.* The Donaldson series of two novels is available: *Rite of Passage* and *Rite of Marriage.*

This is a link to Barbara's website to view all of her books
http://barbararaue.ca

www.ingramcontent.com/pod-product-compliance
Lightning Source LLC
Chambersburg PA
CBHW040228220526
45473CB00001B/160